KEEPING THE PEACE

KEEPING THE PEACE

A Police Chief Looks at His Job

by
Herbert Jenkins

HARPER & ROW, PUBLISHERS

NEW YORK, EVANSTON, AND LONDON

FIRST EDITION

LIBRARY OF CONGRESS CATALOG CARD NUMBER: 72-95967

For my family

Contents

I wish to record here my appreciation to the Anti-Defamation League of B'nai B'rith for their contribution in the preparation of this book.

Introduction

Respect for the law is the policeman's Hippocratic Oath. It is his guiding star of survival in a democratic society. The newest police recruit can never hope to move forward as a career policeman without this fundamental principle. Respect for the law. But in a democratic society laws are not handed down from above but are made, and *unmade*, by men. Laws come and go and men come and go but the democratic process continues—firmly embedded in law and order. Policemen are society's full-time employed agents to uphold the law and preserve order.

Day in and day out, for the past forty years, I have been a witness to drastic changes in law enforcement. Many of these changes have come from within the police departments themselves. Many more of them have been forced upon us from without. Concurrent with the social revolution within the larger community have come changes in the police departments of the nation. They have brought a change in attitude, in ways of doing and thinking, and an increasing understanding that the old methods will not suffice for the future.

I do not think the future looks bleak. We in law enforcement are beginning to respond positively to the great changes taking place in America. In far too many instances, unfortunately, the response to these pressures has been an unlearned and violent one; in some cases we have been guilty of gross indifference. At other times we have been uncertain, perplexed, and confused about what our response should be.

However, modifications in law enforcement *are* being made and it is the purpose of this book to give the general public as well as the officer on the beat some awareness of the continuing changes in police practices and modern methods of law enforcement.

KEEPING THE PEACE

1

Rookie Policeman

When I joined the Atlanta Police Department in the early thirties I was issued a badge, revolver, blackjack, and Sam Browne belt, and sent out on patrol with a senior police officer. After one week of "training" I was a full-fledged policeman and on my own.

By today's standards this is an almost unbelievable way for a policeman to start out, for in the Atlanta Police Department, as in other metropolitan police departments, recruits are put through intensive mental, physical, sociological, and psychological testing as well as many weeks of training before beginning their police duties.

In the thirties the Atlanta Police Department, like its counterparts throughout the nation, had few procedures and fewer recruitment standards for the hiring of police personnel.

My grandfather, Jasper Jenkins, had been the sheriff in a

county in middle Georgia before I was born. Our family had moved to Atlanta in 1924 and my father, because his father had been well known in the field of law enforcement, had little difficulty, because of these credentials, in joining the Atlanta Police Department. Although I was the eldest of six children in the family, I was not old enough to join the police force. In those days an applicant had to be twenty-three years old and of a specified height and weight.

Life in the country and the business of farm chores had taken up most of my time and, although now seventeen years old, I had been able to complete only the ninth grade in school. It was necessary for me to get a job and help out with the finances at home.

Since I could not be a policeman, I went to work as an apprentice automobile mechanic. I had an uncle who had left Henry County, Georgia, some years before and was now parts and service manager of the Ford agency in downtown Atlanta. In those days working for an automobile agency, particularly a Ford agency, was as glamorous as working for a computer company today and was in the hub of activity of a bustling city.

My first day on the job a customer asked me street directions to a location in another part of the city. To my great dismay I realized that I didn't know the location or the names of any of the streets he was inquiring about and was not only unable to direct anyone else but could not find my own way around without having to ask directions of someone else. That very day I began memorizing the names of streets and learning the locations of various places around town. If I wanted to become a police officer I had to know my way around town not only for my own benefit but in order to assist others.

Working at the Ford agency brought me into contact with many interesting and important people of the city. It soon became my job to teach people to drive. Back then many of the people who were buying cars had driven nothing but a horse or had confined their motoring to unhurried Sunday afternoon drives in the country. But the streets of Atlanta were becoming congested as more and more people acquired automobiles, and driving for the unskilled was becoming risky. Quite often the sale of an automobile by the company was concluded by the fast-talking salesman assuring the wary buyer that the company had a man who could teach anyone to drive. Of all the dangerous situations that I was to face in the years ahead of me as a career police officer none would be more hair-raising or dangerous than some of the happenings I encountered trying to instruct courtly, nineteenth-century gentle-bred Southern folk in the seemingly unfathomable mysteries of operating and mastering "that infernal machine."

I began my duties as an Atlanta police officer in October, 1931. Several months earlier my father had been killed on a skidding motorcycle that struck a utility pole on a rain-slicked street. My grandfather had been killed two years before I was born when he was cut down in a shoot-out with a trapped escaped prisoner.

I was married now and had the responsibility of a family and was anxious to begin my career as a police officer. It was now my time to uphold the family tradition.

The police have a strict code of taking care of their own. Because of my father I was permitted to join the police force and given preference over others when a vacancy occurred.

Remembering my own early frustration at not being able to join the force when I had a burning desire to become a police officer, I have been particularly alert to this problem with others. Often when a young man with the right potential and character has come to me and said that he wanted desperately to be a police officer, but could not because of age

3

or school requirements, I have tried to find him a place in the nonpolicing aspects of the force: the fingerprint bureau, records department, or other office sections of the department. Many of these young men have gone on to become outstanding police officers.

But if the police have a close family-like code it does not always work in society or the department's favor. Too often it fosters the worst possible kind of recessive inbreeding. It too often entrenches the surly element and places in line of promotion relatives and cronies of someone "with an inside." It builds up an image of the cracker-barrel loiterer who has "got it made" and is only hanging around to pick up his retirement check when his time has been served.

In the thirties in Atlanta and throughout the South it was helpful to join the Ku Klux Klan to be an accepted member of the force. This was your ID card, the badge of honor with the in group, and it was unfortunately often an allegiance stronger than the policeman's oath to society.

Not every member of the Atlanta force belonged to the Klan but those who did not had very little authority or influence. The Klan was powerful in that it worked behind the scenes with certain members of the Police Committee and the City Council. A well-liked and respected member of the department who was not a Klan member could still get promoted through the ranks if supported by the Klan. But as he owed his rank to the Klan he could never defy them for fear of his job—and his life. The Klan was a kind of Mafia in dirty sheets.

Anxious for advancement, I joined the Klan along with the others of my generation of police officers. As a matter of course the new recruits were gathered up one night and carried to Stone Mountain to take the pledge of allegiance in front of the traditional flaming cross.

This was the extent of my association with the Klan. When

4

I was told that new members would be assessed $15 for bed sheet "uniforms" I had nothing further to do with them. I already wore a uniform and had no intention whatsoever of covering it with a bed sheet. I suffered no reprisals at the time and no one in the department gave any notice—or so I thought.

In January of 1933 Atlanta was in the grip of the worst stages of the depression. A police cadet's job in those days was grim. I had not thought that I had put on the police uniform to run down relatives of nameless bodies found dead from hunger in the streets or to be besieged by frightened men and women possessed by fear and pushed beyond the point of human dignity where they begged to be arrested to gain a warm night's rest and a hot meal. The situation became so acute that it was necessary for the city to make available the facilities of the city auditorium for the hungry. With the aid of various religious and civic groups the city operated a soup kitchen there for several months. When I was not trying to referee a domestic quarrel often turned violent and bloody because of the forced hostility of the times, I was usually directing people—who often had spent their last dime in search of hope in their journey to the city—to the city's soup kitchen. I made many lifelong friends during this time because as a police officer I somehow represented hope to these hungry and frightened people.

In the early sixties, when those times had all but been forgotten, I found myself making a speech at one of the more affluent service clubs of the city. I was trying to convince a skeptical audience that it was the responsibility of all—yes, even the police—to be involved in social helpfulness if the times in which we live demanded it; and I concluded by saying that the police were involved in the social changes of the day and were depending on the aid and assistance of people like themselves to support our endeavors. I sat down to polite applause and felt that perhaps I had not communicated what I felt as well as I would have liked.

Upon leaving the meeting one of the members stopped me and congratulated me on what I had said. It was a man I had known for a long time but had seen little of in recent years. He told me that my speech had brought back the memories of thirty years ago when I had taken him and some others to the city's free soup kitchen. He said that in the years between he had been very successful in business, as I well knew, and had had little time for concern with the problems of today. But my talk had caused him to start thinking and remembering ...

I told him that I appreciated very much what he said about my speech but what I really appreciated was his reminding me of the incident that I did not recall and that I respected him greatly as a man for having done so. Some days the job of being a policeman is filled with great rewards.

I had read in the Atlanta *Constitution* that as a depression-oriented economy move it had been decided to replace the $175-a-month fireman who chauffeured Mayor James L. Key with a $75-a-month police cadet. I wanted this job badly.

I went to see Mr. Henry Arnold and asked him if he would talk to Mayor Key about appointing me to the job. Mr. Arnold had been an old customer at Ford. I had seen to the servicing of his model T and had attempted to improve his driving skill when the Ford Motor Company had shifted to the model A. Mr. Arnold had never done too well with the model T and the transition to the model A had been somewhat harrowing. One uneasy day I had been instructing him in Atlanta's Grant Park (home of the famous Cyclorama and a favorite driver-training area for me at the time because of its many curving uphill and downhill obstacles and its lack of busy traffic) when suddenly, in attempting to change gears on a steep incline, Mr. Arnold had choked the motor and we had rolled back into a large oak tree. After a few minutes to recover Mr. Arnold said to me:

"Herbert, I don't think I will ever be comfortable with anything but a horse!" It was more than my usual discretion that made me agree with him, most emphatically.

I failed in my attempt to make Mr. Arnold proficient in driving the model A, but he did not fail me when I requested him to speak to his old friend, Mayor Key, about me. I was appointed to the job as the Mayor's driver and assigned by the Police Department to his office. The first thing Mayor Key said to me was that if I was half as patient a fellow as Henry Arnold said I was I could handle the job just fine.

It was a challenging job and I worked day and night trying to do the best job possible. I was painfully aware of my lack of schooling and began reading nights on the subjects of history, political science, and sociology.

Any concept which I had difficulty understanding I would, in unhurried moments, ask Mayor Key to explain to me. This he would do with unfailing interest and great patience and would suggest further reading in books which I got from the public library or borrowed from the Mayor's own wide collection of books and other reading material.

Mayor Key was one of the best-educated and liberal minds in politics at the time. Always outspoken and frank, he had jumped into international fame in 1931 while attending a United States Mayors' Conference in Paris.

"Prohibition is abominable," he said, "but the people will change it one of these days. Seeing a country like France, where there is no prohibition, has convinced me that crime in America is due, in great part, to the 'dry' laws."

Upon his return to Atlanta Mayor Key faced a political uprising from a coalition of labor, church, and outraged Prohibitionist groups. They secured the necessary petitions for a recall election and the Methodist bishop barred him

7

from attending services at Grace Methodist Church where he was a member and had taught the men's Sunday-school class for many years. When this occurred Mayor Key began conducting his own services at the Paramount Theater in Atlanta and taught a Sunday-school class attended by some 2,500 people. By the sheer force of his personality Mayor Key managed to rally the business leaders of the city to his side and win the election. The election was a rebuttal to the Prohibition forces in the capital of Southern Protestantism and they never forgave or forgot, or readmitted him to church.

This election was a significant prelude for the city of Atlanta. It proved that Atlanta, under intelligent and vigorous political leadership, would in the future be a business-oriented town (as opposed to a city such as Birmingham that was heavily labor dominated) and would be open to the development of new ideas even to the point of rejecting, by referendum, Prohibition before the passage of the 21st Amendment to the Constitution. It also foretold something else.

One of the essential aspects of my job as driver to Mayor Key was to check daily with his secretary and find out what appointments the Mayor had for that day. I was routinely checking one day when I discovered that the Mayor had a Sunday afternoon appointment at a church on Mitchell Street. I was not familiar with the church and when I checked the city directory I concluded that it could only be a Negro church. I figured there must be some mistake and brought this to the Mayor's attention. No, there was no mistake. Friendship Baptist Church was celebrating a special occasion and the Mayor was to be the guest speaker. If Mayor Key was aware of the blank look on my face he gave no notice.

When we reached the church that Sunday the Mayor greeted the minister, the Rev. Mr. Carter, and the other dignitaries who were present. He then turned and introduced them all to me. It was the first time in my life that I had ever shaken hands with a Negro.

Mayor Key strode inside greeting everyone as he went. He seated himself behind the pulpit and the preacher began introducing him. I had found an inconspicuous seat in the rear of the building and observed the proceedings with an uninvolved and critical air. As the minister warmed to his subject, however, I became keenly interested in what was being said. I was greatly impressed with the minister's remarks and marveled at his erudite language and learning. It was a memorable experience.

Some weeks later a group of Negroes called on the Mayor at his office. There were some others, but those I recall being in the group were: C. A. Scott, publisher of the Atlanta *World*, A. T. Walden, the prominent attorney, and the Rev. Martin Luther King, Sr. They spent some time with the Mayor and after they left he called me into his office. The Mayor was sitting at his desk looking out the window toward the downtown section of Atlanta. He explained to me that the purpose of the delegation's visit had been to make a request of him that the city hire Negro police officers.

I was thunderstruck at such a suggestion and began to protest but the Mayor cut me off. He told me that such a thing was not possible for the present and would only be possible in the future when the Negro people and white people had been educated to the idea. He said that he had no doubt that such a thing would occur in the future and, turning around in his chair and looking me straight in the eye, said it would occur peaceably only if those in positions of authority at the time had the wisdom and ability to make it so.

He went on in great detail to explain to me how all this had come about, of how the white politicians had attempted to circumvent the intents and purposes of the Constitution by

9

enforced segregation. When the recall election of 1932 occurred it had been a general election, and for the first time in years Negroes had been able to play a decisive role in the election of a mayor. In previous elections candidates had run in the Democratic primary, which by state law was a "white primary," and, since there was no Republican party in the South at that time, selection of the candidate in the white primary was tantamount to election. The black citizens of Atlanta had supported the Mayor in the recall election and as a result segregation forces in the state legislature had just changed the term of office for mayor of Atlanta from four years to two. Without Negro support the segregationists felt sure they could defeat Mayor Key in the white primary election of 1934 (wherein he ran and was re-elected).

As a cold political fact, Mayor Key told the Negro delegation, any attempt to grant their wish would mean certain defeat for himself and the probable election of a staunch segregationist. They had left his office realizing all too starkly the political reality of the Mayor's words.

If this settled the matter—and I thought at the time the idea of Negro police was just not possible—why did Mayor Key spend so much time explaining to me in great detail what had occurred? If it was settled it was settled. It was years later before I realized that the matter was far from settled. I also realized that the Mayor, as an old man then, was trying to educate me and the city of Atlanta for the future.

Since then on many long, work-filled nights, the Mayor's words have come back to me and I now realize that the two central premises that he spoke about at that time and reiterated to me again and again were all too true: it was morally right and just that Negroes be allowed to serve as policemen but that would be brought about only through the education of both races and the emergence of the Negro as a political power.

10

By the time I came to work for Mayor Key he was a national figure with many friends and political associates throughout the country. He attended all the Conference of Mayors meetings and was the leading organizer of the Georgia Municipal Association. On all these trips he insisted that we travel by car. His schedule was heavy with meetings and appointments at what seemed to me ever-widening distances on the map. When we traveled we had to travel fast.

Fortunately traffic then was not what it is today, but then neither were the highways. Detours, washouts, and billowing clouds of dust were ordinary driving hazards.

The Mayor liked to have a friend or two come along with him on these trips when possible. One afternoon we were traveling through Florida north from Miami when a gale-force wind materialized out of the northeast. An old friend of Mayor Key's was along on this trip—asleep in the back seat with his feet propped against the right rear door. The Mayor, alert as always, was riding in the front with me. The gentleman in the back seat somehow dislodged the door, the wind got behind it, and lifted it gently as a feather right off its hinges and sent it sailing out into the sand dunes in a matter of seconds.

"Mr. Mayor! Mr. Mayor!! Have you got the door? The door, Mr. Mayor!! The door? ? ? ?"

When I managed to stop the car the Mayor turned to his friend and said calmly, "Al, this is a helluva way for you to be treating city property. I will have to insist that you make proper restitution for the damage." The poor man did not know he was being put on by the Mayor, for he had done nothing but fall asleep in the back seat.

The remainder of the trip homeward was made with the rear door tied on with a bunch of loudly colored neckties. The door was replaced and fixed properly by the gentleman, who never was too sure how responsible he was for the accident.

11

Mayor Key never let the man in on the joke.

In accompanying Mayor Key on these trips I had the opportunity to observe closely the operations of many American cities large and small. We attended the World's Fair in Chicago in 1934 and many World Series games. It was a broadening experience for a country boy out of the deep South.

Mayor Key made several trips to Warm Springs, Georgia, to visit Franklin Roosevelt both before and after he became President. The two men had much in common and enjoyed each other's company greatly.

Traveling by automobile in that era was never dull. We were rushing back to Atlanta late one evening when we came upon a wreck. Two cars, traveling in opposite directions, had collided. The two drivers had got out and were engaged in a heated discussion. Their automobiles had the highway completely blocked.

When no amount of horn blowing could get either driver to move his car and clear the way, I set the emergency brake firmly and started to get out of the car. The Mayor wanted to know what I was going to do.

"Tell these jerks a thing or two!" I replied angrily.

"I think you should stay where you are," he said solemnly. "We already have two fellow citizens standing in the middle of the roadway making fools of themselves. I see no reason to bring further disgrace to the Republic by increasing the number to three."

In 1936 Mayor Key was embroiled once again in a hot campaign for re-election. His administration had been in the great liberal tradition. He had supported President Roosevelt vigorously and instituted many New Deal–type programs to help bring Atlanta out of the great depression. He had antagonized his old foes by insisting that Sunday afternoon movies and baseball were harmless forms of recreation for

12

the many people who had but one day off a week in which to see a ball game or go to a movie.

One day I reported to him on a newspaper article quoting the president of a young men's civic organization as saying that Mayor Key was a cantankerous old man who should be sent into retirement by the voters. The Mayor reflected upon the article thoughtfully and then replied quietly:

"The trouble with that group is that they act too much like eager young jackasses earnestly striving to become old farts."

While I was impressed by the Mayor's rather colorful appraisal I was concerned with his lack of interest in making an appeal to this group and winning their political support. I knew that the opinions they expressed were gaining wide appeal and, unless their challenge was met head on, the issue of a tired, testy old man too long at the political mill would gain support.

However, no amount of arguing could convince the Mayor to accept the challenge. It was an exhausting campaign and the Mayor was weary and in failing health by the time it was concluded. I had forebodings of disaster at the polls.

The Mayor faced tough opposition in the person of a vigorous Atlanta lawyer with a great deal of zest for politics. It was a classic campaign wherein the old had to make way for the new. When the ballots had been counted the Mayor was defeated and the voters had elected William B. Hartsfield to the highest elective office in the city.

A phase of my police career had ended. From the time of the election until Mayor Key's term ended I was too busy helping the Mayor, by now a very sick man, vacate the Mayor's office to reflect upon my own future.

It was a dreary day in January, 1937, when I reported not to the Mayor's office but to the police station to answer roll call. I wasn't sure that I would have a job. In political upheavals such as this policemen on the losing side often find themselves out of a job. Somehow I managed to stay on. Probably in the confusion of the new administration I was merely overlooked, and the chief quietly gave me a routine assignment. I thought at the time it was the better part of discretion not even to inquire.

Throughout the last years of the decade I remained a rookie policeman. Other men who had come into the department at the same time or later than I did were moving up in the ranks. I was associated with a different political administration and didn't keep my Klan dues paid up or attend meetings, and this was brought to my attention upon several occasions. All things considered, I thought myself lucky just hanging on.

During the years of World War II I began to observe in Atlanta at first hand some of the things I had learned during my service with Mayor Key. Atlanta as a railroad hub felt the full influx of military personnel during the war. Often troop trains seemed literally stacked on one another at the depot. Many times there was friction between white police and Negro servicemen from the North unused to Southern ways of segregation. Once a Negro Marine sergeant was forced to wait in the "colored" section of the waiting room; although he voiced his objections to the policy nothing serious happened. Incidents of this nature were beginning to occur more frequently. As a police officer I was required by duty to enforce the law and the law then was segregation. But what I saw told me that once the war was over a profound change would take place. You could feel it in the air.

My service as a rookie policeman was a time of learning. To all new policemen I stress this point over and over again. Be alert and aware. Observe and remember. Whatever you learn in the first few years as a policeman will markedly influence your entire career. A new policeman must apply himself and work hard to learn the job of being a *good* policeman. He will probably never again work as hard. Regardless of the assignment a rookie policeman should give every task his best effort.

We have come a long way in police training since I joined the force. The days when a young man could step onto the street as a policeman on the day that he was sworn in are fortunately gone forever. The intensive training and schooling which a young man undergoes now before becoming a police officer is the most scientific schooling that we know about.

Never again will the policeman have the time to learn and observe that he will have as a rookie. The best advice I or anyone else can give a policeman is to use this time well. Apply yourself to your assigned task. More to a policeman than to anyone else in any profession I say: learn while you can. The future is full of surprises. You never know whether what you learn in the beginning will or will not be of use later.

2

Chief of Police

I became chief of the Atlanta Police Department in February, 1947, at a time when the serious problems dealing with the racial question had finally to be faced. For many years they had been allowed to fester in an atmosphere of neglect and indifference, but with the end of World War II they could no longer be ignored. The policy of legal segregation was at last under attack.

The Supreme Court of the United States had ruled the Texas White Primary Law unconstitutional in 1945. Denying the Negro his right to vote was no longer legal. Negroes would now be voting in all municipal and state elections and, as all city employees must realize sooner or later, every person who is a voter is ultimately his boss. No chief of police can ignore this fact and long survive.

Only a few weeks before my election (by the City Council) as chief of police, as commander of the uniform evening

17

watch, I had been called to the scene of a disturbance at a house in what was then a white residential section in the inner city.

A Negro man, just returning from service in the army, had bought a house in the neighborhood with federal assistance under the GI Bill of Rights. Although the neighborhood was all white, it adjoined an all-Negro neighborhood. It seemed a natural site for Negro expansion at the time.

The white residents of the neighborhood, however, were having no part of Negro expansion into their neighborhood and the night before my visit a brick had been thrown through the living-room window of the man's house. A note had been tied to the brick: "Nigger, you can't live here!"

As I arrived on the scene the Fire Department was in the process of putting out a fire set by some unknown persons on the back porch of the house. I talked with the man who had bought the house and he told me that he was being continually harassed and threatened by telephone and through the mail by individuals who identified themselves as Klan members. As a result his wife was afraid to stay in the house with their small children, and he had decided that for the moment at least he must rent out the house to a white family. The notes on the loan for the house were $50 a month while the rent he was to get for the house amounted to $35 a month; even so, he felt that it would be too dangerous for him and his family to live in the house at that time.

In due course other Negroes bought houses in the section and there were the same general disturbances and threats until several Negro families established themselves there and the tension subsided. Yet with an expanding Negro population in search of a place to live it was obvious the problem was a lingering one. It continued to be a police problem because as Negroes tried to find living space within the city they were constantly met by a solid wall of white resistance that often

18

became violent and menacing. The white community insisted that they objected to Negro expansion only because it made property values go down and that if one Negro moved in the area would become all Negro. The fact of the matter was that, since the existing Negro neighborhoods occupied the core of the inner city, expansion into adjoining neighborhoods meant they were moving into areas that were already becoming run down. White resistance created a situation in which a Negro family could not move alone into a neighborhood because threats and violence intimidated a lone family in an all-white neighborhood.

Thus the seeds of decay of the inner city were planted. The economics of the situation forced the Negro to edge out from the core of the city section by section. Unlike the white person, a Negro could not "jump over" these narrow battle lines into a newer section of town. He was trapped and in the decade of the sixties he would explode out of his entrapment.

How different things might be today if it had been possible at that time to open up areas other than run-down neighborhoods to Negroes, to have headed off at the start the momentous rise of the ghettos within our cities. But hindsight is clearer than foresight and at the time there were few people or agencies seriously concerned about seeking solutions to this problem.

The high crime rate in the Negro sections of the city was appalling. At the same time, and because of decades of Klan interference and domination, morale and discipline within the Atlanta Police Department were a disgrace. Charges of brutality were constantly leveled at the police by both press and public. Concerned civic and religious groups and an aroused press clamored that something be done about the situation.

It soon became apparent to me that if Atlanta was to have a police department that could respond properly to all these

19

pressing problems a complete reorganization of our methods and operation had to be the first order of business.

To find out what was being done in police administration elsewhere, I immediately began an inspection tour of police departments throughout the nation. I was firmly convinced that in order to implement modern police practices we had to establish effective training methods for police officers.

It was my fondest dream, and the first order of business, to establish a first-rate training school within the Police Department. I have probably devoted more time and energy to the implementation of this training school than to any other project I have ever undertaken for I felt then, and feel just as strongly today, that a police department *cannot* be an effective force in the community without the most modern and thorough training methods and techniques available.

As I look back upon it I think that my visit to the major metropolitan police departments in the nation must have been one of the strangest tours of the times, for wherever I went, whether in the North, South, or West, I encountered little but apathy and indifference to the problems I raised.

Police departments in the postwar forties were generally housed in old buildings that at best could be described only as medieval monuments to tradition and self-centeredness. They were generally staffed with overweight cops who thought I was crazy to be concerned with the problems of training, the enlistment of Negro police officers, and police brutality. On a tour of a large police department in the Middle West, when I inquired whether the department had any problems of police brutality particularly toward Negroes the captain of the watch replied:

"Absolutely not! The 'coloreds' have a way of settling things among themselves and we don't interfere—unless of course things get out of hand, and then we go in with guns blazing and a hell of a lot of men."

20

In the Northeast, while touring late at night, I asked to see the city's Negro section. The police officer accompanying me looked at me as though I had lost all my marbles.

"I wouldn't think of going into that area with just the two of us this late at night." When I asked why, he looked at me incredulously and did not answer. I thought then that if there was any area in a city where a policeman was unable to go alone something was very wrong indeed.

I had been led to believe by the press that brutal police methods were confined to Klan-dominated Southern police departments. It was in fact the criticism of the local and Northern press which had been partly responsible for instigating my trip to police departments throughout the country. I had begun the trip with feelings of inferiority, but I returned to Atlanta with the knowledge that we were in no worse shape than anybody else.

In most departments the charge of police brutality was a joke and completely ignored. Negro policemen were employed in most if not all Northern police departments and in border areas such as Louisville, Kentucky, but in no instance did they comprise over 1 percent of the total manpower of the force. In no department, with some notable exceptions, did they hold rank above that of patrolman. Police training, if it existed at all, was on a primitive level.

My tour to the various police departments reinforced my view that much needed to be done. I was determined to move forward.

The only agency that I could turn to was the Federal Bureau of Investigation. Even then this organization and its eminent director, J. Edgar Hoover, possessed a legendary pre-eminence in the field of law enforcement and I was convinced after my tour that this respect was well earned.

On the other hand, during my travels about the country I had heard police officials give the FBI hell for just about everything. The main complaint was that the FBI was always poking its nose into civil rights cases involving the charge of police brutality and it was the general police view in those days that the FBI was somewhat left wing!

No kidding. Not only in Southern police departments but generally throughout the country the hostility expressed by local police departments toward the FBI centered around what they considered a too-liberal stance by the bureau with regard to what was thought to be a purely local police problem—racial policies and practices. This as much as anything convinced me that if I was to get assistance in modernizing the Atlanta Police Department I had to turn to the FBI.

I felt like the dean of men at State College calling on the president of Harvard when I went in for my interview with the FBI director. I had spent much time and given much thought to the preparation of what I wanted to say to the director which would enhance the possibility of gaining assistance from his organization. I had thought I would encounter a quietly efficient, stern lawman. My preconceived image did not quite match the actual person, however. When I entered his office, Mr. Hoover jumped up and greeted me cordially—bouncing around the room with the enthusiasm of a teen-ager. He lit into the subject of law enforcement and talked for two hours straight. When I came out of his office I had received a thorough lecture on what was wrong with law enforcement in the United States. Mr. Hoover was aware of the deficiencies and needs of local police departments and pledged the full cooperation of the FBI in helping the police in Atlanta modernize.

In May, 1947, the FBI Training School conducted a three-month course in Atlanta for the members of the Police Department. This was at the time the largest training school ever conducted. Following this extensive training program, we set up in Atlanta a modified FBI training school of twelve

22

weeks' duration which all city police recruits who came into the department thereafter would be required to attend.

Regularly after that Atlanta police officers attended the FBI National Academy in Washington, D.C., and took the twelve-week course there, designed for instructors. They learned how to teach courses in identification, investigation, report writing, and firearms.

With an effective training program that could be built upon, added to, and modified in the future, the sole remaining obstacle to the training program was the organized opposition within the Atlanta Police Department.

This opposition came from two sources. Members of the department who had been on the force thirty or forty years hooted at the idea of going back to school. There was then no mandatory retirement age for police officers and men in their seventies were still policing. There was an assistant chief in the department who had joined the force six years before I was born!

I proposed that the department have a mandatory retirement at age sixty-five. Although this was in keeping with general business practice, we had to overcome a court case to make the ruling stick.

The other source of opposition was from the police union, which was not a union at all but in fact a thinly veiled cover for Klan membership. I do not think a police department is a place for a union any more than the army is, although my views are now somewhat more moderate than they were in the beginning. But, faced with a union dominated by the Ku Klux Klan, I knew it had to be destroyed quickly if a professional police organization was ever to be built.

The Klan members brought more pressure to bear. Those outside the department attempted to get us to let up on the union. I issued an order barring Atlanta policemen from union membership and prohibiting any union meetings or other such functions from being held at the police station. The union leaders challenged this order in court but the courts ruled against them. Thus, backed up with a court order, union members had the choice of either leaving the union or leaving the police force. All except a few diehards chose the former course but those who did not either retired or resigned.

Now that two of the biggest roadblocks to modernization of the department had been removed we could go forward.

But the thorniest problem of all was the recruitment of Negro policemen. In the battle with the union this issue had always been hidden just beneath the surface. Here I encountered the pervasive and corrosive power of racism and was for the first time subjected to the stinging epithet of "nigger lover."

Obviously this issue, if not properly resolved, could tear the department to pieces. All my experience in police work told me that we could not bury our heads in the sand and refuse to meet this challenge. We had to have Negro policemen in the department and we had to do the job right or otherwise all the reforms that had been made would come to nothing.

What brought the issue to a head was the lack of law and order in the Negro community. In a society of legal segregation there was no problem. There was a white police force to enforce the law for white people. But Negroes were *outside* the legal structure of society and a kind of law of the jungle prevailed both within the Negro community and in the white community's relations with it.

Only when the Negro edged into white society did the white man's law and his policemen become involved. If a white man raped a white woman the legal system dealt with him. If a Negro man raped a Negro woman *maybe* a report was made. Only if a Negro man raped a white woman did the

24

law intervene. Then the Negro was dealt with by the courts —if he made it to the courts alive.

But the high incidence of crime in the Negro community threatened the white community. Thoughtful people, both white and Negro, sensed the danger to the whole community if this condition continued unattended. The situation had to be remedied. The press, along with civic and religious groups, favored the employment of Negro policemen as a means to that end.

Practically the same group that had called on Mayor Key in the thirties now called on me! Now that Negroes could vote in the mayoralty election they were registering their people in increasing numbers. They had a growing list of complaints about their status in the community but none caused more wounds or acute abrasiveness than the relation of the Negro community with the police.

Dr. Rufus Clements, president of Atlanta University, and a distinguished educator in the country, told me:

"I am just plain tired of going downtown and being told by the policeman on the corner, 'Okay, boy, you can cross the street now.'"

Mayor Hartsfield and several influential members of the City Council were on record as favoring employment of Negro policemen. Alderman Ralph Huie (a cousin of William Bradford Huie) had introduced a resolution calling for the employment of Negro policemen but the entire council had let it be known they would vote for the resolution if and when the chief of police recommended such action. They were not about to vote for this radical idea unless the person responsible for making it work would assure them it would work.

My main concern was providing professional law enforcement for all the citizens of the community. The time when the Negro could be denied his rights as a full citizen had run out and one could no longer cling to the concept of segregation. Segregation was now no longer legal and it was my job to enforce the law.

Segregation was not legal. On the other hand, it was impossible to have an effective police department at war with itself over the race problem. Time was needed to allow the members of the department to adjust to this new development.

It was decided to call for a public hearing on the matter. Whenever there is need for a tough decision that is not going to be popular it is helpful to call for a public hearing. This gives time not to procrastinate but to work out a plan for an effective transition.

Talking about Negro policemen helped to dispel the strangeness of this new idea. Both sides had ample opportunity to make their views known. Many people in the white community were unaware of the degradation suffered by the Negro until they heard or read the eloquent testimony of the leaders of the Negro community. Those who testified against the proposal were asked how they would deal with the problem. To the last one they had nothing constructive or positive to suggest. They were just against what was being proposed.

The public airing gave the press the opportunity to report the hearing and editorialize. Ralph McGill, then the distinguished editor of the Atlanta *Constitution*, wrote some telling articles in favor of the proposal.

While the issue was being publicly debated we had time to devise a workable plan. We knew that many white people had very real fears of the Negro as a person and we assured them that the Negro policemen would arrest only Negro persons. This was a large concession to white fear and on the face of it seemed to give assurance that segregation was not being abandoned entirely. This was a glaring inconsistency, of course, but the idea of Negro policemen at the time was so revolutionary that the end justified the means. I felt that

26

in time things would work themselves out—once we got things moving.

This was the big rub. The City Council, upon my stated and public endorsement, had authorized the employment of eight Negro policemen. I well knew that if these eight men were to be effective they must be of the highest caliber obtainable. We spent two months interviewing and selecting the eight who were finally employed.

The new recruits had to be trained properly and for this job I selected Captain E. B. ("Beavo") Brooks for the job. Beavo was a native Atlantan who had been in the department all his adult life. He was liked and respected by the members of the department—at the time he was probably the most admired member of the force. His popularity was only a partial qualification for the job, however. He was also color-blind.

Beavo had grown up in a white neighborhood in Atlanta that bordered on a Negro neighborhood. Many of his childhood friends had been Negroes. His family had been neighborly with Negro families. He told me that when he was a child and went to the store for his mother she would instruct him to go to the Negro woman who lived behind them to see if she needed anything. In the same way when their Negro neighbor was on her way to the store she would stop off to visit and bring back Beavo's mother's items from the store. There was a good deal of this kind of neighborliness, helping back and forth. With this background Beavo was well equipped for the job ahead of him.

In the beginning it was decided, as a precautionary measure, to provide a separate precinct station for the Negro policemen, and the Negro YMCA on Butler Street was used for this purpose. It was also decided that the Negro policemen would leave their uniforms and police equipment at the Y when they went off duty. This was a practical measure for the protection of the Negro policemen themselves. Above all,

27

we were afraid of incidents which might jeopardize the whole program. A lone Negro police officer going off duty in his police uniform would have been a sitting duck for Klansmen and both Negro and white hoodlums.

But I was concerned that the Negro police officers might have difficulty maintaining their identity as police officers during this early period since they were reporting to the Y instead of to the police headquarters and were not even allowed to wear their uniforms when going to and from work.

In talking with these new officers I stressed the fact that in spite of their temporary housing arrangements they were full-fledged officers and should act accordingly. I urged them not to let these less-than-perfect conditions negatively influence their desire and ambition to do an outstanding job and move ahead in the department. When I concluded, one of the young officers spoke up and said he would have no adjustment problem because when he was a boy he had wanted more than anything to be a Boy Scout. His church had finally been able to organize a unit and secure uniforms for the boys but the young Scouts, like the new police officers, had not been allowed to wear their uniforms away from the church. The officer told me that one of the reasons he had wanted to be a Scout was so he could wear the uniform around town as he had seen the white boys doing. He had been denied that but at least he had known that he was a Boy Scout and in the same way his selection as a policeman was for now the most important thing.

It was at this time that I fully realized the job of chief of police of Atlanta, Georgia, brought with it responsibilities for two separate cities: one where Boy Scouts wore their uniforms wherever they wished and one that required them to leave their uniforms at the church. I was determined not to shirk my responsibilities to either.

So it was a sunny Saturday afternoon in the spring of 1948

when the first Negro policemen began their duties on the streets of Atlanta. Mayor Hartsfield and I followed along behind the two officers who began walking their beat up Auburn Avenue. It seemed to us that just about the entire Negro community had turned out for the occasion.

At first there was total silence from the thousands of spectators as the officers began walking their beat. They walked for about two blocks in this continued silence, the spectators staring in wide-eyed disbelief. It was as though they could not believe what they were seeing. Suddenly a stout, elderly woman ran out from the crowd and grabbed one of the policemen, shouting and gesturing wildly at the crowd. The crowd began to respond, cheering and jeering. They closed in on the officers and marched along in front and behind them up the street. The occasion of the first Negro policemen on the streets of Atlanta was being celebrated by a parade!

Despite Klan intimidation and other long-standing opposition to Negro advancement in any sphere, it was the determination of certain civic leaders in politics, in the press, and on the police force that made possible the hiring of Negro policemen in Atlanta.

After the obstacle of employment of Negro policemen had been overcome, a strong challenge developed within the Negro criminal element threatening the effectiveness of the Negro police officers. The employment of Negro policemen had been predicated upon the assumption that such employment would help bring more law enforcement to the Negro community and help combat the spiraling crime rate within the community.

Negroes in Atlanta had suffered badly from lack of protection. The police, the courts, and the white community in general had been indifferent far too long. During this period of indifference roughhouse bullies pretty much had things their own way in the Negro community. I recall one big bully in particular who loudly proclaimed all over town that no Negro cop was going to lay a hand on him.

I remember one incident very well. Captain Brooks was called late one Saturday night to a disturbance at a beer hall on Decatur Street. When Beavo got there a crowd had gathered around the entrance and was pouring out of places up and down the street. Beavo had previously called for a patrol wagon and it arrived on the scene at about the same time he did. Before he could make his way through the crowd there was scuffling around the entrance to the beer hall and the crowd fell back. Beavo then could see what had drawn the crowd. The smallest Negro policeman on the force, Officer J. D. Hudson, had the big tough by the back of the belt and was marching him out of the beer hall and through the crowd. Beavo immediately had the patrol wagon move some five blocks up the street, making it necessary for the policeman to march his man in full view of all the gawkers gathered for the fracas. The officer did so and placed his prisoner in the patrol wagon without difficulty. Beavo said the scene reminded him of a western movie in which the sheriff, alone and outnumbered, at the end subdues the villain and dramatically marches him off to the pokey.

The lesson was not lost on the bystanders. There was still hostility but little *overt* hostility thereafter. There were instances when a brick or a bottle would come sailing out of a dark alley but more often than not the spunky Negro policeman gave chase and captured his man. Within a year's time the Negro policemen had brought law and order to the Negro community and had proved themselves as outstanding police officers. The Y quarters were abandoned and the group was moved into main police headquarters. They still worked as a separate unit, however, and were confined almost entirely to the Negro sections of the city.

Their greatest accomplishment was in providing justice for the law-abiding citizens of the Negro community. Crime among Negroes during the first year of the employment of Negro policemen was reduced by one half. For the first time in the city's history a sizable portion of the population was being afforded proper police protection.

The success of Negro policemen in Atlanta was due primarily to the character and dedication of the Negro policemen themselves but was also due in part to training in modern law-enforcement methods and the enlightened leadership of Beavo Brooks. Brooks's high standing with the members of the force was invaluable in carrying the new officers into the department during those critical years.

By the time the whole department moved into a new building in 1959 Negro officers had been promoted through the ranks and were working in the detective department. At this time all vestiges of a segregated force were abandoned and the restriction of arrest on the basis of color was dropped. Even before this time, however, Negro policemen in the ordinary line of duty had handled situations in which Negroes and whites were involved.

In 1968, at the time of the report of the President's Commission on Civil Disorders, 20 percent of the members of the Atlanta Police Department were Negroes. Incredibly, this was the highest percentage of Negroes on a police force of any major city in the country. It was one of the few which at the time had Negro police officers involved in decision-making policies of the department. Obviously a ratio of 20 percent was not good enough for Atlanta or anywhere else. More will be said later concerning recruitment problems which all police departments face today.

Few things caused more controversy at the time than the employment of Negro policemen. It was seen by many as the first crack in the solid wall of segregation. Several old friends, men I had known since the days of Mayor Key's administration, stopped speaking to me.

There were also political implications in the issue. An influential old-time politician told me shortly after the employment of Negro policemen that Mayor Hartsfield would be re-elected for another term of office. This turned out to be true, and in the next election he received 90 percent of the Negro votes.

And the issue wouldn't die. When the final restrictions on Negro policemen arresting white persons were officially lifted, some twelve years after the first employment of Negro police officers, an irate citizen called me late one night demanding to know how I would feel if my wife were arrested by a Negro.

"Not very chipper," I replied. "It would be a little discouraging after all these years to know that my wife had violated the law."

3

Segregationists Versus Integrationists

There is nothing more native to Atlanta than playing golf. Since Bobby Jones' heyday in the twenties it has been the most popular form of recreation in the city, and with a rather mild winter climate many enthusiasts play the year round. It was therefore most fitting that the first of many challenges to segregation would arise on the tranquil green of Atlanta's golf courses.

The city's public golf courses had always been reserved for whites. The only course available to Negroes was a private course, small and not very well kept up. A group of Negro golfers wanted to play on the city courses and had filed suit in federal court to desegregate them. Mayor Hartsfield met with the Negro leaders and began planning a strategy that would open the courses to Negroes by means of a well-worked-out plan and in a hopefully peaceful manner.

Silly as it might appear to us today, elaborate planning was necessary to bring about the peaceful integration of the city's golf courses in the fall of 1955.

"I would plow up all those golf courses and plant 'em in peas" before he would see them integrated, bellowed Marvin Griffin, Governor of Georgia. With sentiment such as this emanating from the highest political power in the state the difficult job of complying with the law of the land was made much more difficult.

Emotionally the majority of the white community in the South, in Georgia, and even in Atlanta agreed with Governor Griffin's feeling. The Negroes must not be allowed one foot in the door and the iron curtain of segregation must not be breached.

Until they stopped to think about the situation. How would *anybody* play golf in a pea patch? There were private white clubs in the city and in the suburbs, but not near enough to accommodate all the whites who wanted to play. To turn the golf courses into pea patches certainly would be like cutting off your nose to spite your face.

However bitter the pill, closing down the golf courses would not be an acceptable solution for the people of Atlanta. Not in a city where they were in the habit of getting up at four-thirty on Saturday morning to beat the rush to the courses.

Mayor Hartsfield, myself, the head of the Parks Department, and the City Attorney met several times to discuss the matter. We talked individually with various Negro leaders: A. T. Walden and Donald Hollowell, prominent local attorneys, William Holmes Borders and Martin Luther King, Sr., influential religious leaders, and several Negro businessmen. The Negro leadership was agreeable to any plan that would desegregate the golf courses without incident and agreed to make no move to integrate the courses until the city had an opportunity to work things out. It was therefore up to the

34

leadership of the city government to come up with a workable solution.

Mayor Hartsfield had many conferences with leaders of the business community of the city and they considered various solutions to the problem. There was no great enthusiasm for desegregation but there was general agreement that we should follow a course in the best interest of the continued prosperity and good name of the city. Seen in this light, the business leadership understood how a posture of outright defiance, with its ensuing strife, would be foolhardy and not in their or the city's best interest.

It was my task to do a similar selling job with the police and park personnel. We held meetings at the police station in which all aspects of the question were thoroughly thrashed out. We discussed the legal question and the implications of defying a court order. Disregard for the law could quickly lead to anarchy and violence. As police officers we could not be a party to defiance. There was some sentiment for shutting down the golf courses. This was a negative approach and for that reason we had decided not to take this path. We wanted to move Atlanta forward not only in the field of race relations but in all areas, and you could not have progress in one without progress in the other. Good race relations were a vital part of Atlanta's future. Everyone began to understand what was involved here and to accept the decision. I have always believed that a good police officer will perform an assignment much better if he is aware of the reasoning behind the job he has been given to do.

Once the problems were examined and a plan of action worked out in discussions with key personnel, the process was repeated with the officers assigned to patrol the park areas. They could do a better job, and indeed did a better job, when they understood the issue.

Mayor Hartsfield hit on the idea of desegregating the

courses on Christmas Eve of 1955. He felt that this was a good time for action on an issue that was not what could be called overwhelmingly popular. The fact that the Mayor came up with such a suggestion is a pretty good indication of how much thought and discussion had gone into the resolution of this problem. The Mayor and I drove around the course that afternoon, observing the situation. It was a fine golfing day and, as prearranged, several Negro foursomes played on each course crowded with white golfers, without incident. Our preparation was paying off handsomely.

(It was the holiday season and most people were too involved with their own yuletime activities to pay much attention. The situation was well in hand but the police maintained a careful surveillance of the park areas for several days. Fortunately there were no incidents.)

That night Mayor Hartsfield stopped at my home, where a Christmas Eve party was in progress. Most of the people gathered there were outside the city government and had been unaware that the golf courses were to be desegregated that day. They seized the opportunity to confront the Mayor. Mayor Hartsfield immediately sized up the situation and began a lengthy discussion of what had occurred this day, how it had come about, and how pleased he was that things had gone so well.

There was some undercurrent of resentment within the group over what had occurred and some mild objections to integration in general were offered. That is to say, they were mildly expressed. No doubt the sentiments would have been more strongly expressed had the circumstances been different.

The Mayor was equal to the occasion. He went into great detail to explain the series of events that had led up to the day's developments. His method was to supply as many facts as possible in the hope that facts would supplant feelings on

36

this very touchy subject. For several years it seemed that all social gatherings ultimately ended up discussing the "problem." It was a deeply emotional question, one that divided families and separated long-time friends, but the talk, talk, talk was compulsive and could seldom be quieted by the most determined host or hostess.

This Christmas Eve party was like so many others. But Mayor Hartsfield handled the situation impressively. He stressed the illegality of segregation. We were not doing this because we wanted to but because the courts had handed down rulings on the issue. If we tried to resist in an illegal manner we would be in the position of encouraging the Klan and other such outlaw groups to take the law into their own hands. We had to stay on top of the situation. We could not allow the situation to go unresolved and come to a head, causing resentment and pressure on both sides and possibly leading to direct conflict. As mayor, he was not going to stand idly by and see his city torn apart by the race issue.

Mayor Hartsfield stressed that Negroes who played golf were law-abiding citizens and not troublemakers and that playing golf was after all a sport, not exactly a social affair. To ward off any kind of disturbance the Mayor told the group that he had ordered all the locker rooms at the golf courses closed down. Anybody could play golf, but no one could take a shower afterwards. Again, in retrospect, such action appears absurd but at that point in time it was just the kind of reassurance in the right area that white Southerners needed to help them accept the facts of desegregation.

From this experience I believe we learned two things: that careful preparation can bring about peaceful desegregation and that it is necessary to offer the white community some concession in return for its support, even if that appears absurd to some and wrong to others.

With each further Negro demand there was a growing

37

stiffening of white sentiment. Next time it would not be as easy as it had been with the golf courses.

"Next time" was not long in coming. The bus boycott led by Dr. King in Montgomery in 1955 and 1956 had its effect throughout Southern cities. Negro leaders all over the South felt their integrity and influence had to be put on the line on this particular issue. As a result, segregated seating on municipal transportation systems was a sore issue with them. Also as a result of Dr. King's Montgomery protest, the segregationist political leaders were determined not to give an inch.

On January 9, 1957, without warning (never before had the Negro leadership in Atlanta embarked upon a course of this nature without letting us in on it), a group of Negro ministers boarded a bus in downtown Atlanta and sat in the "white only" section of the bus. The driver left his route immediately and drove the bus back to the garage, whereupon the Negroes got off and departed.

There was a state segregation law which stated that all seating arrangements on municipal conveyances were segregated. State officials on every level were constantly calling me on the telephone demanding that the law be enforced. The transit company—faced with what amounted to a near insurrection on the part of the bus drivers—also was calling wanting to know what to do next. Time was desperately needed to try to work something out.

Mayor Hartsfield was on the phone in one of his "jumping up and down" calls. I called them this because in moments of crisis it was necessary to get a good grip on the telephone when he called to keep it from jumping up and down.

The Mayor was right on top of the situation. He had scheduled a meeting for the following morning with business leaders and transit company officials. He was thinking in terms of testing the validity of the law in the courts. We needed the cooperation of the Negro leadership. This was my assignment.

I telephoned the Rev. William Holmes Borders, leader of the ministerial group, and asked him if he would mind being arrested. The Rev. Mr. Borders, a man of wide intelligence and vast understanding, replied that he was not happy at the prospect and would have some difficulty explaining it to his congregation.

Then he asked me exactly what I had in mind. I told him that a suit could be filed attacking the legality of the segregation law and in light of recent events I was confident the federal court would declare it void. This maneuver was necessary to get the state government off our backs. For at that moment state authorities were threatening to enforce the law themselves if there was a repeated attempt at integrating the buses. Mr. Borders agreed this would only heat up an already emotional situation and do great harm. As long as the city and the transit company were committed to working in good faith toward the desegregation of the buses, once the segregation law was disposed of, his group was willing to make no further attempts at integration. In order for the law to be challenged in the courts there had to be a test case—those in violation of the law had to have a case made against them.

"Would you and your group care to come down and be arrested?" I asked.

There was a long silence. "Now, Chief, you know it would be much more effective if you sent the Black Maria to pick us up," was the reply.

I asked him the time and the place and dispatched a white and a Negro officer to handle the situation. Mr. Bill Howland, then the *Time-Life* representative in Atlanta, went along and wrote an article about his ride in the first integrated paddy wagon in the South.

In due course the federal court held the segregated seating law to be null and void and the city's transportation system was desegregated peaceably. Everybody heaved a sigh of relief. We had played for time and used the time granted us for constructive action. The whole community had won uninterrupted transportation service, for there took place no boycott as in Montgomery. The Negroes had cooperated with our strategy and received what they desired. Everybody should have been happy.

But the state government, now embarked on a frantic "segregation forever" policy, was mad as hell. They were spending vast sums of money and employing enormous legal aid to defend every nuance of segregation to the end. This stance on the part of the state riled the increasingly restive Negro community. Dr. King's victory in Montgomery had aroused the will of the Negro college youth. Sit-ins had begun in many sections of the South.

Spelman College for Women, Morehouse College, Clark College, and Morris Brown College are predominantly Negro schools located in the city of Atlanta. All these colleges plus a theology school are a part of the Atlanta University Complex. Atlanta University is one of the largest Negro institutions of higher learning in the world. Students at Spelman and Morehouse decided to lead a protest march and confront the state government with a list of grievances at the state Capitol. The day chosen for the march was May 17, 1960, the sixth anniversary of the Supreme Court's 1954 decision outlawing segregation in the public schools. When word went out that the students planned to march, groups of irate whites came into the city from God knows where. Both groups were determined to make a stand to show their strength.

The state Capitol building, resting on the crest of a hill in the heart of downtown Atlanta, faces downhill in the direction from which the students would march from the west side

40

of the city. The day of the march the building was guarded by some 500 state troopers armed with billy clubs, tear gas, cattle prods, and shotguns much as if it were a medieval fortress under siege. In truth, they would not have minded at all if blood were spilled that day to preserve the "Southern Way of Life."

It required no genius to realize that Atlanta was a city teetering on the edge of violence. All efforts to have the students call off their march failed. Lonnie King (no relation to Martin Luther King), the student leader, told me that they were going to march but would not attempt to enter the Capitol grounds if the Governor or someone in the state government would meet with a group of them. I contacted the head of the state patrol and suggested that it might be well for the Governor to meet with a delegation of the students. He told me that he would have to check it out with the Governor. When I called him back later in the day he said the decision had been made not to receive a delegation or allow anyone to enter the building or even set foot on the grounds. At the urging of Mayor Hartsfield two prominent Atlanta businessmen talked with the Governor and urged him to change his mind—but to no avail. Thus all our efforts to get someone in all the state government to sit down and talk with four college students failed. The march was on.

The students left the university that afternoon in an orderly column of twos. We had police stationed all along the route. There was no trouble. We had worked out in advance with the students the line of march as far as the Capitol. We still hoped that the students might change their minds and simply march through the city avoiding the Capitol entirely, for they were as aware as anyone else of the danger of the situation. The Governor and other high state officials had issued statements literally daring the students to hold their protests there. A large group of angry whites had gathered on

41

the Capitol grounds and the state police had made no effort to dislodge them. When I reached the scene I received word that the marchers had not turned away and were approaching full steam.

We gathered in the wide intersection in front of the Capitol, the "segs" and state troopers at our backs. One last attempt had to be made to avoid senseless bloodshed. The Atlanta *Journal* and various wire services recorded the scene this way:

The students had been singing as they marched up the street to the Capitol but as they confronted the vast array of state police and jeering bystanders the singing stopped and the column hesitated momentarily in a state of confusion. Chief Jenkins confronted Lonnie King at arm's length.

"You are walking into trouble, Lonnie. Turn them away from the Capitol."

King politely refused. The tension heightened.

A student in back of King suddenly jabbed his fist into the air. "We're going to the Capitol," he shouted.

A rumble of assent from the column of marchers backed him up. Jenkins drew himself up straight and summoned all the authority his voice could muster. "Lonnie," he said. "This is an order from the chief of police. *Turn here!*"

There was a long silence. No one moved or spoke. Finally, King turned without a word and led the demonstrators down another street toward the Wheat Street Baptist Church.

Much had been at stake here: good race relations, Atlanta's prestige before the nation and the world, police authority, the Negro cause, the rule of law and order, and the safety and possibly the lives of the marchers. Up until that time it had been the most difficult moment I had had to face since the period of desegregation had begun. Today this incident reads like ancient history. Was there ever a time when public officials would not talk to students and escaped having their

42

offices invaded? When a young Negro leader was more concerned with the safety of his followers than proving a point? When police could still threaten and thus control demonstrators? When segregationists dared gather in groups and spew hatred? There was such a time and it wasn't so long ago. It just seems that it was a long time ago.

Some of Lonnie King's followers told him that he had been "Uncle Tommed" by "whitey." What they did not understand was his realistic political leadership—and his courage.

Some public officials said that these problems could be settled—in time. What they did not understand was that there was no time.

I cannot recall a period when I felt more apprehensive about the future than I did following this incident. An ugly confrontation had been avoided, but only a fool could not but wonder about the next time and the time thereafter.

I was the hero of the day. People who had been previously critical of how we had been handling the racial situation were now congratulating me on keeping the Negro in his place while others demanded we take on the state government in a frontal assault. The police were being praised by both sides for their handling of the situation. This is an unusual result of *any* police action.

What really bothered me was that so many people refused to learn anything from the incident. I had the strong impression that many felt all further demonstrations could be handled with the same methods.

On the contrary, it appeared to me that the incident indicated anything but the possibility of a hardening of attitudes. The white community was going to have to go much further in meeting Negro demands. Negro leaders were going to have to press their demands or else lose their leadership in the movement.

It was also a time of approaching political change in Atlanta. After serving almost continuously as mayor of Atlanta since 1937, Mayor William B. Hartsfield announced that he would not be a candidate for re-election but would retire from office at the end of his term in January, 1962. Mayor Hartsfield was in his way just as colorful and tenacious a politician as his predecessor, Mayor Key. He had taken a lively interest in everything that affected the city and had worked day and night to protect its interests and good name.

This extraordinary Southerner had provided the city of Atlanta with wise and able leadership at a time when most of the South was under the spell of a segregationist blight as devastating as the boll weevil. He had created in Atlanta an atmosphere of racial tolerance that gained the city a national and international reputation in this regard, and under his leadership the city had grown in every facet of its development. But not without cost. Mayor Hartsfield was regularly denounced by members of the state legislature, and the city of Atlanta suffered at its hands because of its moderate racial stance. The main north-south expressway through Atlanta was delayed many years because the state government thought the city of Atlanta should be punished for being what it considered "radical." And in a thousand other ways the state government would go out of its way to give the back of its hand to the Atlanta city government and its mayor.

One of the tactics Mayor Hartsfield always stressed was the importance of keeping the business community informed about what was going on in the Police Department. Through the years of working with Mayor Hartsfield there were several things I learned about working with the power structure (a nebulous group which everyone talks about and no one can define) within the city.

When I first became chief of police I accepted all invitations to speak at every civic and professional club in the city, for I well knew if we were to be successful in modernizing the Atlanta Police Department I would need the solid support of the business leaders of the community. Without their unqualified support the reforms could never have been successfully carried out. It was the same with the great social revolution going on in our midst.

Whenever I or one of the men in the department spoke, we tried to emphasize the importance of law and order and point out how the Police Department was having to undergo certain changes in order to meet the challenges of changing times. We had some success, but far too often after a civic meeting we would be approached discreetly and told that all this social welfare business was well and good but what really needed to be done was "to crack a few woolly heads."

The era of the sit-ins put quite a strain on the Police Department's relationship with the power structure. Groups of students would go through the city "sitting in" at segregated lunch counters in drug and department stores. When this happened the manager would usually announce that the counter was closed and turn the lights out, whereupon everyone would get up and leave. A short while later the manager would reopen the counter and keep it open until another squad of students entered and the process was repeated. There was continual confrontation and jawing back and forth but no violence. But the situation was tense. As the sit-ins continued, the police came under increasing pressure to arrest the "sit-inners." Some managers, rather than close their lunch counters, would call the police and demand that the sit-inners be locked up. They based their demand on the Anti-Trespass Law—one of the many laws passed by the state legislature as a subterfuge for enforcing segregation. Earlier in an offhand comment I had stated that the trespass law was probably constitutional only if it was not used to enforce segregation. I received more criticism for that comment than any other I can recall, which taught me a lesson

45

about offhand comments. Judges informed me in pointed terms that it was not my place to go around passing judgment on the constitutionality of the law. I was told the police were supposed to enforce the law and were negligent in their duty if they failed to do so.

Frankly the police had grown weary of fighting over this matter of segregation and saw little point in operating on the basis of an elaborate set of state laws which would collapse like a crumbling house of toothpicks before the onslaught of a huffing and puffing federal judiciary.

The truth is that the police were no more pleased than anyone else about some of the changes taking place within the community and often thought how nice it would be if we could hold onto the status quo. In this way, it was thought, our problems would go away; yet unlike everyone else we in the department were charged with the responsibility of preserving law and order, however difficult that task might be, and we were convinced that continued efforts to circumvent what the federal courts had clearly ruled to be the law of the land would only destroy our democratic system. Therefore, although under great pressure to do otherwise, the police refused to go along with any further charades enacted to defend segregation to the end. As a result, when most of the store managers eventually realized they could not count on the police to enforce segregation and allow them to continue operating in a segregated manner, they closed down their lunch counters.

This had one good effect. It removed the possibility of direct confrontation between sit-inner and lunch counter operator over whether or not the sit-inner could eat at the lunch counter. As a consequence the possibility of violence was lessened.

The city of Atlanta was in the most critical period it had ever faced. During the early stages of the sit-in demonstra-

46

tions Dr. Martin Luther King, Jr., was arrested for the first and only time in his home town while leading a sit-in demonstration in downtown Atlanta. Although he was quickly released on bond along with the others, Dr. King refused to sign his bond and leave jail. When he finally relented and did so, he was arrested shortly afterwards in De Kalb County, Georgia, on a traffic license violation charge and sent to state prison!

The segregationist mentality knows no subtlety. It was believed that Dr. King could be placed on a chain gang and all problems would evaporate. However, in a famous telephone call presidential candidate John F. Kennedy and his brother, Robert Kennedy, intervened and Dr. King was released. Some say the course of history was altered.

Be that as it may, the sit-in situation in Atlanta, which was the main cause of Dr. King's being in jail, was still unresolved. Lunch counters remained closed. In addition, the Negroes had launched a boycott of downtown merchants. Things had never been this way in Atlanta before.

Why did this situation continue? There were many reasons but I think mainly it was because a large segment of the business community decided to adopt a wait-and-see attitude. Their continued success in business depended upon public acceptance of their policies, and a whale of a lot of protest was being received by letter, phone, and public statements from a public insisting it would never do business with any firm which gave in to the outrageous demands of the Negroes.

There was confusion among the business people. Many were just local managers of chain store operations who were instructed to do what the prevailing climate of opinion favored, but under no circumstances to get caught out on a limb as an identified integrationist. Everyone was afraid to make the first move.

And there were all the most influential state people including the Governor and the United States senators counseling the store owners not to give an inch. They advised that the United States Congress would never pass a public accommodations law, and even if this vastly unlikely event occurred their stores would never have to bow to the Negroes' demands because "how a man operated his business was none of the government's business."

Private business was being charged with racism and the protestors were demanding that right and not racism should prevail here. The power structure, like the community, was divided on the issue. Business was off and shoppers complained that going downtown was a nuisance because of the difficulty of having lunch. The rigidly segregated restaurants did a booming business. The lunch-counter operators complained bitterly that if they were forced to desegregate everyone should have to desegregate. They were being discriminated against. It was true: a public accommodations law that would have applied to everyone equally was what was needed but at the time it was not forthcoming. The situation dragged on, seemingly insoluble.

Ultimately the power structure brought about a settlement of the lunch-counter problem. Ivan Allen, who was to succeed Mayor Hartsfield, acting in his capacity then as president of the Chamber of Commerce, managed to bring all the parties together at the conference table.

When Richard Rich, president of the largest department store in the Southeast, announced to the group that Rich's would, under certain conditions, reopen its lunch counters on an integrated basis, a settlement was reached and the stores involved in the dispute quickly agreed to follow suit.

Clearly, this is not the best example I could have given of the need for cooperation between the police and the power structure in a city, for it is not a simple issue. The point is, however, that the two groups must make every effort to work together while the police must diligently try to serve the total community.

We in the Police Department were convinced then that had we continued to try to enforce the policy of segregation we would have been party to bringing the city of Atlanta and its citizens into disrepute.

4

Militant Youth

From the first day that I became chief of police I have attempted to maintain a continuing dialogue between my department and the press. Needless to say, I have not always been successful, but generally speaking the relationship has been a harmonious one.

The press and the police have many interests and obligations in common and I have always tried to seek these similarities rather than the differences. We are both responsible to the total community—not just a segment of it. We both must zealously guard our integrity: the press must report what it sees and hears or else make itself liable to the charge of not reporting the whole truth. In similar fashion the police must stay within the letter of the law while keeping the press informed.

The police always seem to be in the news and have to learn to live with the press. Keeler McCartney, police reporter for the Atlanta *Constitution*, has been at his job nearly as long as I have been at mine. There must be some kind of double record here, not only for endurance in our jobs but also for our endurance of each other.

The thing that Keeler and I have always had in common is a reverence for the facts. This respect has often led us into dangerous situations when we felt impelled to observe at close hand an event which we might better have avoided. Once we were almost attacked at a Klan rally.

Keeler had driven out with me to a park where the Klan was holding one of its "public" rallies. I was observing and Keeler was doing his job as a reporter until someone in the crowd spotted us and alerted the others. A good-sized group began insulting us, so we decided to depart. By the time we reached the car we both were at a near gallop, with a large contingent of Klan members in hot pursuit. We got into the car to make our getaway but the car wouldn't start. Needless to say, we spent quite a few restless minutes until I succeeded in summoning assistance over police radio.

The most remarkable incident I know of in which the press and the police worked together for the good of the community occurred in Atlanta when the public schools were desegregated in 1961.

Much depended upon the orderly desegregation of the Atlanta public school system. The agreement on the desegregation of the lunch counters rested on the peaceful integration of the public schools. Complicating this situation further was a mayoralty election which coincided with desegregation of the schools. And last but not least there were our eternal foes of the no-no-no school—not one inch will be given here. For months these people had been insisting that the schools in Atlanta could not be peaceably desegregated.

But two events occurring beyond the political influence of the city of Atlanta made the issue easier for our orderly desegregation. One was the series of rowdy demonstrations which took place with the desegregation of the public schools in New Orleans in 1960. That spectacle, carried by television throughout the world and viewed in most of the living rooms in the country, had made a deep impression upon Atlanta's leaders and had shown all of us how *not* to desegregate the schools.

Commenting on this incorrect approach, Mayor Hartsfield vowed that the Atlanta city government would assume a different stance, for Atlanta was a growing, thriving, industrial center that was "too busy to hate."

Another event that helped us greatly was the desegregation by the federal courts of the University of Georgia in Athens in January of 1960. Again television made visible a streak of unabashed ugliness within the Southern soul. We in Atlanta were determined not to show our backsides to the world in this manner. The desegregation of the University of Georgia by two Negro students had cracked the monolith front of the segregationist leadership in the state. They could no longer point an accusing finger in our direction when the first integration of the schools in the state of Georgia had already taken place outside of Atlanta.

Nevertheless, while the old forces were battered they were still unbowed. Day by day as September approached we got word of dozens of would-be troublemakers coming in from as far away as Texas and California. It soon became apparent to us in the Police Department that if we did not formulate a plan of action some very ugly incidents might occur to mar peaceful desegregation of the schools.

All the training we had experienced in our years of operation went into preparation for this ordeal. We knew that if the department could withstand this big test our future effectiveness as adequate leaders for law and order within the community and the state would be greatly enhanced.

53

As the opening of school neared, the situation grew specifically threatening. In addition to a large segment of the KKK located here, the city's hoodlum population was swelled by seemingly the largest and most ill-assorted contingent of racists and bigots ever to assemble in one place.

Within this group were known "bombers" and a local company had recently reported to us a sizable theft of dynamite. If the city was to uphold its good name the police had to be in command of the situation at all times.

The superintendent of detectives and his assistants set up a task force of detectives to keep an eye on all the troublemakers. The task force built up an impressive dossier of "crackpots" and kept watch on them twenty-four hours a day. Wholesalers and local suppliers of commercial explosives and firearms were furnished with pictures of these individuals and asked to inform us immediately of any contacts or dealings they might have with them. These merchants, as anxious as we to preserve Atlanta's good name and reputation, cooperated 100 percent.

The initial desegregation plan was for nine Negro children to enter four previously all-white high schools. A police task force of superior officers, patrolmen, traffic policemen, and detectives was set up for each school. Each group was organized at its assigned school, beginning their duties the day before school opened in September. They had blueprints of all the school buildings and learned the location of key points within each building. They spent time getting acquainted with the personnel at the schools so that by the time school opened every police officer knew on sight every individual who worked at the school to which he was assigned.

In addition to the task force on location at each school, a special force was on standby alert at the central police station and could be at any one school within fifteen minutes.

Several days before schools were opened, Mayor Hartsfield

called a meeting of the Atlanta press—newspapers, radio, and television—at the city hall. It was anticipated that some ground rules for dealing with the press could be set up. It had already been decided to keep all unauthorized persons off school grounds on opening day. Now we were trying to work out guidelines for the fourth estate. In addition to the local press, some three hundred national and international correspondents streamed into Atlanta to cover the school integration story.

Fortunately every press representative in attendance at the meeting pledged his cooperation in supporting whatever was necessary to help preserve law and order. The press in New Orleans and other places had been severely criticized for contributing to the chaos of school integration in those cities and the news media were well aware of this complaint.

For integration of the schools in Atlanta the press agreed to stay within specific bounds off school property and it was agreed that no reporters would be allowed in the school buildings during school hours. The object was to make this day as near like any other school day as possible, for indeed that is what it was.

Much has been said about the role of the press, particularly television, in relation to the desegregation battles in the South. With the exception of the Negro leaders themselves, probably no group has been more seriously vilified than the television medium, for obvious reasons.

To racists who streamed into Atlanta during integration of the schools the glare of the television lights was a withering presence. How could they carry on their cowardly and underhanded deeds facing the television screen and finding themselves pictured in homes all over America?

The press, for its part, provided excellent coverage of the event without unduly exciting the students with the vast array of personnel and equipment.

Mayor Hartsfield set up a gigantic press room in the council chamber at city hall and had telephone lines and teletype machines installed so that all members of the press could file their stories promptly. We at the police department hoped there would be no stories. At least not the kind that most of the correspondents were accustomed to filing while covering integration at Southern schools.

Television stations in the city made available free air time for those of us who had direct responsibilities in bringing about peaceable integration. Dr. John Letson, Superintendent of Schools, appeared on television and urged parents and their children to accept what was happening in the school system with good grace, for it was properly considered just the beginning of another school year in Atlanta.

Mayor Hartsfield and other community leaders also went on the air to plead that Atlantans have respect for the law and make integration work. I, too, went on the air and assured parents that the police were working twenty-four hours a day to keep the hoodlums and troublemakers away from the schools and that I was confident we could do so. I felt it was important to let parents know that it would be safe for their children to attend school. This was also necessary for there was a group in the city vigorously urging that parents keep their children away from the schools, saying that it wasn't safe. I had to reassure the parents that there was no danger —and I had to be positive that I could back up what I said. Of course, none of us could be absolutely sure. We gathered frequently at police departments for conferences to discuss the dangers of the situation.

Our detective superintendent would report on the whereabouts of all the "kooks" and would-be dynamiters in the city, and the four commanders of each school task force would report on the situation at their respective schools and offer suggestions. The vast influx of troublemakers had us all concerned. It was decided to send policemen to *all* the high schools on opening day, since it was possible there might be trouble even at the schools not actually being integrated.

We were also determined that absolutely no one but teachers and students be allowed in the schools or on the grounds. A troublemaker could conceivably attempt to pass himself off as a parent if some control wasn't maintained. The school administration agreed with this decision and cooperated fully. On opening day the faculty and the police would be at the schools and would handle the students. Outsiders would be kept away. I began to feel confident that no potential troublemakers would get very far.

Security for the nine Negro students themselves had to be provided. A police department detective was assigned to drive each one of the students to his assigned school. I instructed every detective to get to know the parents and the students at the school he was responsible for and to submit a written report on the students' integration at the previously all-white schools. It was important for the policemen to know the background of the students involved and for the students' parents to feel they were getting professional police concern. When I read the reports the detectives turned in I was struck by a recurring sentiment of the parents. To the last one they were, if not entirely opposed to their children going to white schools, to say the least, far from enthusiastic about it. They naturally were concerned about their children's safety and they seemed to feel it also might have been better not to rock the boat; but each of the children had been carefully selected by school officials and wanted very much for this step to be taken. It was obvious to me that each student had had to do quite a selling job on each of his or her parents to get them to go along with the project. The parents seemed resigned to it only because of the youths' insistence.

Much of what we had been hearing from public officials

and was being discussed discreetly was the opposite view. The prevailing white opinion was that the NAACP, the radicals, and Negro parents were forcing integration of the children. I felt that if these groups would just quit pushing there would be no problem. I felt that such an attitude, particularly in the police department, had to be challenged if school integration was to be a success.

We hit upon the idea, in 1961, of having our police training school hold a special seminar for every man on the force on the question of school integration. Lectures and discussions were held on the entire subject of desegregation and the courts. Each policeman was required to read *With Justice for All*, published by the Anti-Defamation League of B'nai B'rith and the International Association of Chiefs of Police; George McMillan's booklet, *Racial Violence and Law Enforcement*; the 1961 report of the U.S. Commission on Civil Rights; and Dr. Robert A. Matthews' book, *How to Recognize and Handle Abnormal People*.

We bore down hard on the illegality of segregation and its pernicious effects on the Negro minority in our community. As a conclusion to the seminar the men were instructed to write themes listing the reasons why segregation could no longer be maintained.

The exercises leading up to school integration were probably the most successful we ever undertook in changing attitudes on race and desegregation. Fact was substituted for emotional fancy, and open discussions replaced hearsay and whispered innuendo. The prevailing sentiment within the department became: "Why should a bunch of hoodlums be allowed to destroy the public education system in the city?"

Many of the officers themselves had children in the public schools and wanted them to continue their education uninterruptedly, as you might well expect. Thus several months before school opened a change of attitude in the department

58

had taken place. We had done our best to see that law and order would be preserved.

On the day school opened there was only one minor incident at one of the high schools and the police quickly handled the situation. The vast assemblage of press and other news people in the city had little to report other than it was a "normal" school opening in Atlanta in September of 1961.

Now that school desegregation had actually taken place in Atlanta without undue incident, I had opportunity to relax and try to visualize what my department might be called upon to face in the next decade.

The sit-in movement, the first attempt at integration, had made me aware of a new breed of American youth. Observing and talking with the Negro children who integrated Atlanta's schools made me realize that a major concern of the police in the sixties would have to center around the activities of youth. We in the Police Department were going to have to revise our working relationship with young people in our society in order to make ourselves more aware of their needs, desires, and ambitions. What I had experienced during school integration led me to believe the gap was widening between the young and the police and I realized it had to be bridged.

I tried to visualize how this situation had come about. I understood that mobility of the population since World War II had done much to separate the youth of the country from early and helpful contacts with the police. Whereas formerly a child might grow up in the same neighborhood in which he was born, and often his father before him, now families moved frequently from place to place seeking locations in keeping with their rising (or falling) status in society.

Whereas once a police officer might be assigned a beat in a neighborhood and stay in that same area for twenty or thirty years, now policemen are regularly transferred and assigned to various duties in keeping with the organization of a modern, efficient police department.

All these and other factors tend to separate the growing child from any association with policemen in his community unless he gets into trouble. This is no small factor in the crisis in communication between a mushrooming youthful population and the police department.

The traditional association between police and youth in Atlanta had evolved from two long-term practices: having a policeman working the school crossing and encouraging the schoolboy patrol organization. When children walked to and from school in Atlanta there was always a policeman to help them safely across the street at the traffic intersections.

As a young police motorcycle officer I had worked a school crossing for several years. I got to know the people of the community and I learned to know their children. Oftentimes I would ride a child home on the motorcycle and frequently looked out for "strays" on days when their mothers might be late reaching the crossing to walk them the rest of the way home.

But when I became chief of police, Atlanta, like all urban centers, faced a serious traffic crisis. I had often speculated during the war years that once the American economy became geared to civilian needs the influx of automobiles might create a traffic jam that could never be untangled. This was just about what happened. Atlanta streets that had followed what were once cow paths were not built to accommodate the influx of a mass of modern automobiles. New streets had to be planned, old streets widened, and an expressway system undertaken. In the meantime the police had to keep traffic moving as best they could.

Of course the busiest times of the day were rush hours in the mornings and afternoons. The thought occurred to me that if all the policemen who were tied down at school crossings at the peak rush periods could be relieved for traffic duty, we could greatly improve traffic conditions in the city.

Louisville, Kentucky, had faced a similar problem in traffic and had employed women in the neighborhoods to act as traffic policewomen and make the school crossings safe. I was told that the system in Louisville had worked well and that safety at the school crossings had not lessened while traffic enforcement had increased.

The employment of women at school crossings was much more economical than hiring more policemen, and very shortly we, in Atlanta, made the changeover. The women surpassed all expectations for ability and efficiency. They were all mothers with children in the schools where they worked and the city was able to employ them on an hourly basis.

I employed Negro women to work the crossings at Negro schools. Up until this time there had never been police assigned to the crossings at Negro schools. No one seemed to have thought about this part of the problem. The legal counsel of the local branch of the NAACP, A. T. Walden, called me and thanked me for this action. I also received a letter from Walter White, executive director of the NAACP and an Atlanta native, in regard to this matter. They both stated that to their knowledge this was the first time in the history of the South that a police official had ever done anything for Negroes without even a request.

The hiring of women to work at the school crossings was a move that put more police on the streets at the least possible cost to the taxpayer and was a popular and wise move at the time. The unfortunate side effect was that children went through elementary school without ever encountering a male police officer. Here, personal contact was lost.

The school safety patrol suffered somewhat the same fate. One of my greatest satisfactions as chief was derived from

61

escorting school safety patrol members to the national jamboree in Washington, D.C., each spring. For $35 each member of the elementary school safety patrol could go on a four-day train trip to the nation's capital and see most of the historic sites. We always had a large and "spiffy" contingent from Atlanta and won the national trophy many times in the parade down Pennsylvania Avenue. We were the first group from the South that included Negro children.

I recall one year standing in the reviewing stand as our group came by. As always, a large number of representatives and senators were in attendance to greet their home delegations. Our state's leading segregationist congressman was on the platform enthusiastically waving at our delegation as they marched past. As the large group of Negro youngsters passed by he seemed to hesitate a moment and then turned to me and asked: "Are they in our group, too?" When I replied that they were, with consummate political agility he continued waving vigorously.

But the school safety patrol grew greatly. More and more children wanted to go on the annual trip to Washington, which required more and more policemen to accompany and look after them. We had the choice of limiting the group to a select few or discontinuing the jaunt altogether. Much as I hated denying the children this annual event and giving up the trip which was to me a personal pleasure, I had no alternative because of the growing demands on the police officers' time. The trips were discontinued altogether and the operation of the school patrol was taken over entirely by the traffic policewomen who covered the school crossings. They have done and continue to do a great job. But that vital communication between the policemen and the children was lost.

Every policeman in the Atlanta department has always been encouraged to take part in outside civic and church activities. It was felt this could go a long way toward improving police public relations. I taught a teen-age Sunday-school class for many years. I stuck mostly to the basics of Abraham, Isaac, and Jacob. But as the racial crisis came to the forefront and the class members heard the subject discussed by adults they began questioning their Sunday-school teacher, who increasingly felt he wasn't doing an adequate job without trying to bring the Old and New Testaments up to date on this subject.

I found that the youngsters often expressed far more advanced sentiments than their elders. They could also discuss the issue with reason and reflect on the basic Christian principles without becoming unduly emotional.

One of these teen-agers expressed his sentiments better than I have ever heard it expressed before or since. One Sunday morning we were discussing integration. At the end of the discussion there was a period of silence during which at least one youngster pondered its meaning. Then he said, "What you hear nowadays is not what I used to hear. I have lots of trouble these days in getting my beliefs and my prejudices synchronized."

My experience with these teen-agers in my Sunday-school class taught me that the great social problem of our time could be reasonably met and rationally solved.

An incident several months later polarized this widening gulf between the generations in regard to Christianity and race. Police were called to one of the large downtown churches, although this was the last thing we wanted to be involved in concerning this crisis. I decided that Superintendent Jim Moseley, one of the most alert and responsible men in the department, should take this call and observe the situation at the church but not get involved unless it was absolutely necessary.

Several white and Negro youths who were not members entered the church for Sunday services. This particular church was conservative and had not encouraged integration. There had never been a Negro in attendance there previously, which was why this group of students had decided to go there. At the same time other similar groups were visiting churches throughout the city without incident.

This particular church had admitted the group after some delay and a harried call to the police to say that there were Negroes in their church and there was "bound to be serious trouble."

Superintendent Moseley stayed throughout the service and saw no disturbance created by the presence of the Negroes. As the congregation was leaving, a young white church member came up to the visiting student group and told them he was glad they had come to his church, he hoped they had enjoyed the service and that they would come again.

As he continued to walk out with one of the Negroes in the group, the young white church member walked past a pew where an older church member had remained standing at his aisle seat, listening to the conversation and observing what was going on with a critical eye. Just as the white and Negro youths passed his pew, the older church member reached out and pinched the white youth on his backside as hard as he could. Naturally, the young man was highly indignant but the Negroes in the group persuaded him not to engage in angry discussion with his assailant!

So fell another bastion of segregation in Atlanta.

It was often in this period, though, that the police heard the words "there is bound to be trouble." Hardly a day went by that someone did not call to say that if the police did not do so and so or if they did this or that "there would be trouble." I never was able to decide whether this might be wishful thinking on the caller's part or a direct threat. It was perhaps a combination of the two.

In time it became a not-so-subtle threat when the Negroes began to voice it. In the beginning it was the white segregationists' line. Whoever uses it places the police on the spot. Such information cannot always be ignored.

Fortunately, we in the Police Department have come to know most of the leaders of the student movement centered in and around Atlanta University. Two of these who were most active in the student sit-in movement that desegregated the lunch counters in 1960, Julian Bond and Ben Brown, are among several Negroes elected to the Georgia legislature. I foresee both of these gentlemen embarking on long and distinguished careers in government service to the people of their state and the nation.

At first students worked in the civil rights movement as a very disorganized group. Leaders would graduate from college and go on to other endeavors. Other students would move up to take their place in the movement. There was little formal organization.

But in 1960 the group began calling itself the Student Nonviolent Coordinating Committee. This was a coalition of groups that had been active at many Negro colleges throughout the South and the nation.

Along with formal organization came more planning and action, and an attempt by this group to represent all younger Negro activists. Their main concern about this time was the pockets of segregation in public accommodations remaining throughout the South, a continuing source of resentment and bitterness.

Mayor Ivan Allen, elected in 1962 following the retirement of Mayor William Hartsfield, had strongly supported a national public accommodations law, the first elected city or state official in the South to do so. But the law was long in coming and various restaurants in Atlanta continued to maintain segregated business establishments. This was the opportunity that SNCC—or "Snick" as it was now being referred to—needed to keep its organization going and keep its demonstrators demonstrating.

In the spring of 1963 Atlanta was besieged with another flurry of sit-ins. But times had changed. The feeling among the "bitter enders" of the segregationist mystique was that private property was sacred and that, although they opened their doors to the public, it was their right to deny admission on the basis of color to those individuals not of the white race.

Once again the Police Department was caught in the middle of an alarming situation. On the one hand, we faced the demand of the segregationist restaurant owners that we must assist them in enforcing segregation by arresting the demonstrators when they tried to enter the business establishments.

On the other hand, the demonstrators demanded that the police not interfere with their constitutional right of protest. What was the law? In such a muddled situation we asked that before any arrests be made the restaurant owners get a warrant from the courts legalizing such action. The owners could find no judge willing to sign such a warrant and the situation continued at a stalemate with the demonstrators picketing the restaurants. Occasionally they attempted to enter and were bodily barred at the door by the owner and his employees. The situation was tense, but with nothing more serious than a good deal of pushing back and forth. Had the police arrested everyone the restaurant owners wanted arrested, it would have been necessary to erect a stockade to hold them.

As the situation dragged on, SNCC, which up to this point had had lagging membership problems, was gaining hundreds of followers ready to go to jail for their cause. The stubborn white resistance was building up a nearly defunct organization into a viable and effective political action group.

The restaurant owners blamed the press for building up

the Student Nonviolent Coordinating Committee, although the press was merely reporting the happenings. It was mainly the unwillingness of the restaurant owners to accept changes in their old ways that was building up SNCC.

During the weekend of May 4, 1963, in Atlanta things came to a showdown. The Ku Klux Klan assembled in downtown Atlanta to demonstrate for their cause. They wore traditional "uniforms" but no face masks, for this was now prohibited by law.

As evening turned into night, a large group of SNCC demonstrators was marching up and down the street. Directly across from them on the opposite side of the street the Klan members marched up and down. Right in the middle stood the police and an irate citizenry which because of the crush of demonstrators could not get around downtown.

It happened that there was a large delegation of Africans and their aides from the United Nations visiting Atlanta at the time. They had come to town with Morris Abram, a distinguished former Atlantan, to attend a seminar at Atlanta University and to observe a Southern city famous for its good race relations. They could not have been present at a more unpropitious time!

We in the police detail who had been keeping an eye on the situation began to have that "something-has-got-to-give" feeling. Having been involved in this sort of situation for several years, we had come to know pretty well when tension had reached a breaking point.

The explosion began at one of the restaurants being picketed. A very heavy-set buxom lady demonstrator had managed to get into the doorway of the restaurant and wedge herself in so that the only way she could have been ejected was for the men in the restaurant to push against her bosom. This tactic disconcerted the restaurant people and each time they tried to eject her they hesitated. Every time

67

they paused the young lady edged a little farther inside, using what must have been the most extraordinary battering ram known to such "warfare." It was a most effective weapon, and she and several others made it into the restaurant before anyone knew what had happened or could think of a way to prevent it.

The policemen on the scene found it necessary to move in promptly and arrest the demonstrators participating on the charge of creating a disturbance in a public place.

What occurred next caught police off guard and totally unprepared. On a prearranged signal, all the demonstrators gathered around the restaurant and the marchers on the sidewalk went limp and fell to the ground. Several rolled under the police patrol wagons while others blocked the street, which was by this time congested with traffic. The ploy was obvious and successful. It effectively prevented the police from bringing in reinforcements quickly. I was standing across the street with Captain Beavo Brooks and we stared at each other in disbelief that the situation had come to this point.

Our first concern was to get additional policemen to the restaurant area. When this was accomplished, we turned our eyes on the Klan to see what they were doing. Amazingly enough—they were just standing around in a state of stupefaction.

With some semblance of order restored to the street the police began bringing the demonstrators out of the restaurant and placing them in patrol wagons. The demonstrators mostly continued limp, although some resisted.

Grabbing a big white tablecloth one Negro youth pulled it over his face, ran up to a Klansman, stuck his head out and yelled "Boo!"

General pandemonium broke loose. The streets and sidewalks filled with police, protesters, Klansmen, "eyeballers,"

68

and others. Just about this time some of Morris Abram's group from the United Nations, dressed in their colorful attire, came to the scene to observe integration and the democratic process at first hand.

By the time the last demonstrators were hauled out of the restaurant there was a good deal of resistance and fighting back. The police, quite outraged by this time, were hardly docile.

The last demonstrator brought out was the heroine who with her unique weapon had made the big breakthrough. On approaching the photographers she went limp all over and the efforts of the police to get her into the patrol wagon were far from genteel. By this time the reporters were all over the place. Later the story was reported throughout the nation, and we received many letters accusing the police of brutality and violence and of disgracing the city by using sadistic practices on innocent people. A prominent national magazine condemned our handling of the situation in general and our rough handling of the heroine in particular. Our only defense was that the policemen did the best job they could under very trying circumstances.

From this point forward the social revolution was not quite the same. The police were catching it from all sides for failing to handle the situation properly. The international press said we had been too rough and the local citizenry said we had been too lenient. Anyway, we all realized that it was a new beginning.

5

Making Friends
Not Enemies

The middle sixties found all thoughtful people in the United States deeply troubled and concerned. The relationship between police and society appeared at the edge of a dangerous precipice. Disrespect for law seemed to be growing. An already overblown crime rate soared even higher. Was a breakdown of all constituted authority imminent? The question, only a few years before, would have been absurd. In the mid-sixties this was no longer the case.

The press, the power structure, youth—all the concerned "groups of influence" within our society became involved in a determined effort to get at the root cause of the current malaise.

In Atlanta Mayor Ivan Allen was an originator and a catalyst. He was determined to try to do something about the smoldering situation before it reached crisis proportions—an admirable characteristic of all the mayors of Atlanta for whom I have worked.

Under Mayor Allen's aggressive leadership a blue-ribbon group of citizens was empaneled as the Atlanta Commission on Crime and Juvenile Delinquency. Along with twenty-six other able and distinguished citizens who served, Federal Judge Griffin Bell was appointed chairman. Only in Atlanta would a federal judge have been asked to chair a commission of this magnitude. In most Southern communities federal judges were totally excluded from local political and social affairs, and as a result these communities lost the experience and service of their most able and distinguished citizens.

But not in Atlanta under Mayor Allen's leadership. For not only did a federal judge serve as chairman of the commission, but leaders from every segment of Atlanta life were represented on the commission. As a group it incorporated all the various points of view in the city.

Judge Bell appointed a very able attorney, Francis Shackelford, as general counsel, and eight other young attorneys to act as staff for the commission. As the work of the commission went on through several months the burden of much grinding, late-night work which would ultimately become the commission's report naturally fell upon these young attorneys. The finest thing about the commission's work was to observe their intent involvement in the whole problem of crime and their vigorous determination to do something positive about the conditions of those living in urban areas.

Judge Bell divided the commission into six subcommittees: Juvenile Delinquency; Rehabilitation; Crime and Health; Crime and Poverty; Law and Order; and Organized Crime.

The committee members were selected and appointed on the basis of their interest and abilities in their specialized fields. The commission made an in-depth study of all the causes and cures of crime in Atlanta. Judge Bell held weekly

72

meetings with the commission and guided the preparation of a report entitled "Opportunity for Urban Excellence."

Among the commission's significant findings were that crime and poverty were inseparable twins and that one condition could not be improved without improving the other. They were really like Siamese twins, called Crime and Poverty.

The commission recommended that the Atlanta Police Department employ police community counselors to work in high poverty and high crime areas. This recommendation had a twofold purpose: to help improve conditions in these areas and also to improve the image of the police in high crime neighborhoods.

This was a totally new approach to crime prevention and law enforcement generally. In the past the police had made every effort to keep the line between social welfare service and police service separated. However, under the Crime Commission's recommendation, the services in many areas would be combined and thus additional duties and responsibilities would be placed on the police.

There were two courses the Police Department could have followed at this point: (1) to accept the change immediately and carry out the program with our present employees and equipment or (2) to oppose the change with delaying tactics and wait for additional appropriations and personnel before taking any action.

The latter alternative has too often been the traditional police response to change and innovation. In 1961 the then newly appointed Attorney General, Robert F. Kennedy, had tried in vain to create a blue ribbon National Crime Commission to examine in depth the same problems on a national level that the Atlanta Crime Commission had dealt with on the local level. But he had been thwarted by those who insisted that laymen had nothing constructive to contribute to the problem of crime and the problem was better left to trained professional lawmen.

For a while we in the Atlanta Police Department shared this viewpoint, but being on the front line every day of the battle we gradually came to realize that the old methods, whether our own or anyone else's, were not adequate to meet the challenge of changing times.

And, too, because of the great admiration and respect that we in the department had for the ability and integrity of the members of the commission, we accepted the soundness of their recommendations and began implementing them immediately. (This same respect might not have been aroused by a non-Atlanta group.)

We were wary but willing to accept the commission's judgment. We recognized that there was need to offer some social services through the police, for in the past whenever a social worker had been confronted with hostility and resistance while trying to do the job he usually backed off and called the police for assistance. This had been the pattern for years.

We also recognized that to provide this service the police would have to be especially selected and trained to wear two hats: (1) to act and serve as a social worker and (2) when conditions required, to arrest and prosecute law violators.

The Atlanta Crime Commission pointed out the abrasive relations which existed between ghetto residents and the police. One would have had to be blind even then not to realize that such a situation would ultimately lead to violence unless something was done. The commission specifically recommended the employing by the police of community relations officers to work in the ghetto areas.

This and other recommendations of the commission depended on the appropriation of funds from the city, state, or national government to be carried out, but at this time there had as yet been no rioting and there was no money available.

It was therefore up to the Atlanta Police Department to create and carry out a program with existing facilities and personnel. Naturally, as we got into the program money was needed from time to time for special equipment and projects. Mayor Allen was tireless in finding the money, never failing to come up with whatever the Police Department asked for, usually with little or no help from other recalcitrant and indifferent local and state officials.

In January of 1966 we organized the Crime Prevention Bureau as part of the detective division of the Atlanta Police Department, and detailed sixteen police personnel to it, including both Negro and white detectives and uniformed officers to operate it. In so far as there was no money available for hiring the community service officers which the commission had recommended, it was necessary to pull these men off regular police duties in order to run the new unit.

Many people in the department were opposed to this. Their argument was that we were already critically short of police personnel and could ill afford to remove competent police officers from their regular duties to engage in social welfare work!

Others of us shared their feeling, yet we also recognized the magnitude of the wrath rising in the ghetto. Those who opposed this new departure in police work argued that, with the inner city ghettos in an explosive state, what was really needed were more trained police who could control the situation by whatever force necessary. But the questions others of us asked were: Would force by itself be sufficient? How much force? And if we needed more police, how many more?

Whenever changes had been made in department policy there had been opposition within the department itself. There were those who had insisted that a Negro policeman would never be an effective police officer because he was a Negro. There were those who had declared that all civil disobedience must be met with unrestrained force. We had not followed these policies in the past because most of us felt they would no longer work and we felt the same way now. The only reasonable solution was for the police to become "involved."

In spite of this lack of unanimity the Police Department decided to go ahead with the Crime Prevention Bureau unit. It deserved at least a trial attempt. Several suggestions as to what we should call this new unit were made, but we decided to stick with "Crime Prevention" as that was the department's primary aim with this new program.

The Crime Commission had also called for the building of Crime Prevention Centers within the ghetto areas and the employment of community service officers to man them but, as I have indicated, the old bugaboo of insufficient funds prevented this. There were, however, Economic Opportunity Atlanta Centers in many ghetto areas already in operation and more would be built later as the program was expanded. We began operating the crime prevention program out of these centers.

The officers in the Crime Prevention Bureau were assigned to Economic Opportunity Centers in the ghetto areas with special instructions to act as guides and counselors in finding jobs for the unemployed; encouraging dropouts to return to school; assisting in providing food and other welfare services; providing tough, quick, and reliable police service for residents of the ghetto; acting as advisers on good citizenship and making friends for the Atlanta Police Department.

The officers in the Crime Prevention Bureau under normal conditions worked an eight-hour day, except that their workday began at twelve noon and ran until eight P.M.—much later in the case of emergencies. These Economic Opportunity Atlanta, or EOA, Centers in effect became store-front police departments, for all the vital police services of a modern department were available within the ghetto neighbor-hood.

As we have so often discovered in developing modern police procedures, there just are no precedents. We now had a Crime Prevention Bureau, but how did we begin to use it properly?

Police departments have always been available to boys' clubs, Scouts, and other youth groups and this type of activity had gradually been labeled as crime prevention. But the police had never moved into the area so completely before and had never, but *never*, been involved specifically with crime prevention in poor neighborhoods.

Our role had always been to serve as advisers to white, middle-class youths belonging to middle-class organizations run by energetic middle-class mothers and fathers. Here the situation was entirely different. There were no organizations for the ghetto kids to join and in many cases households were headed by a working mother and an absentee father. Some-how the police had to find the way to be of help.

In the early days of the program a squad of Crime Preven-tion Bureau officers would converge on the selected neigh-borhood and go down the streets knocking on doors. They had to get to know the people and have the people get to know them—fast. The people in the neighborhoods did not know about the Crime Commission, EOA, or the Crime Pre-vention Bureau. It was the job of the police to make these people aware of the existence of new agencies placed there to aid and assist them in their lives.

Finding Jobs for the Unemployed

Obviously the police had no jobs to hand out, but they did know where an unemployed person could go to look for a job.

77

Before, if a social worker had told a resident of the ghetto he should go to the State Employment Office to apply for a job, the resident would more than likely never have summoned up the will to go or else would not have known where to go or how to go about it even if he desired to do so. But a policeman who urged him to seek out employment was in a stronger bargaining position than the social worker. His uniform represented authority. It also represented know-how and a certain intolerance for a lackadaisical attitude on the part of the resident. Besides the police officer could take the person to the State Employment or EOA offices in a police car in a matter of minutes.

Once at the proper destination, the police officer could assist in filling out forms and withstanding interviews. He could also cut through red tape, for our officers learned quickly that if their work was to bring results they had to use unorthodox methods and cut corners to arrive at solutions. It wasn't an assignment in which you could go by the book.

People with even minimal training and little education, if they had the desire, usually secured employment. But what were the police to do about the chronically unemployed or those too old and unwilling to return to school for training? The police kept in touch and tried to keep them working at least part time. When requests come in for part-time workers the police know who the person is who is good for a couple of days' work and no more.

We discovered something about the men of the ghetto: they are either young or old. There is no middle age for the man in a poor neighborhood. The man might not be old in years but to see him and talk to him you quickly realize that in body and spirit he is years older than his white counterpart of the same age living in the suburbs.

Finding jobs for the hard core unemployed is the biggest hurdle. At Mayor Allen's continued insistence the city of

Atlanta began opening up jobs in city government to the Negroes of the poverty areas. Rigid, middle-class personnel procedures were set aside if there was any chance the individual could do the job. Again prodded by Mayor Allen, private businesses began programs of hiring and training people living in the ghettos.

Encouraging Dropouts to Return to School

A tremendous effort was made by the Crime Prevention Bureau to get dropouts back into school and keep them there. If sometimes the future did not look too promising for the elderly in the ghetto, we at least hoped to make it a different story for the young. The policeman attempted to identify himself to the youngest residents of the ghetto, for even the preschool child left by his working mother at the day care centers in the area would form an opinion early in life regarding the man in blue. Psychologists told us if a good impression is formed early it will more than likely remain with the child as he or she grows older, but if a bad impression is formed at an early age it takes much more time and effort later to break down this mistrust.

The biggest effort was placed on the school-age child. Most important was getting him into school and keeping him there until graduation. Oftentimes the police would serve as a go-between for the student and his school. Many misunderstandings arose that the police were helpful in straightening out.

For instance: it is a well-known fact that the older kids in these neighborhoods bully the younger ones to the extent that often they are intimidated from attending school. An older ghetto kid who never attended school feels threatened if he cannot force other youngsters to share his feelings and it is a difficult problem for the schools to do anything about these conditions because the mischief is usually done some distance away from the school itself. The police, in the area day and night, are better able to deal with this problem.

Illiteracy in the ghetto is a gigantic problem, not only among those of school age but among adults also. The Atlanta Board of Education has enlarged its adult education program and the police urge adults who must work in the daytime to go to school at night.

A big problem with ghetto youth is that school has no interest for them. They have difficulty in seeing its relevancy to their lives. Statistics bear this out to an alarming degree. From 50 to 80 percent of ghetto youngsters never complete high school. Society is simply going to have to make the school experience more relevant to these youngsters or else all the police work and all the antipoverty work will come to nothing. We have neglected one generation and witnessed the fiery result. We cannot afford to ignore the next.

Youngsters in poverty areas who begin to drop out of school at age eleven or twelve usually go into petty crime as a way of picking up money and a way of passing the time. They begin by purse snatching and coin box robberies. For "kicks" they start drinking cheap wine and getting "high" on glue sniffing. When a kid sniffs glue regularly he is referred to as being "on the bag." (The glue is placed in a paper bag which is held tightly over the face.) As these kids progress, by their late teens they are usually involved in armed robbery and on their way to prison.

What this costs the individual and a society composed of such individuals is impossible to measure. It is staggering to consider. What we are spending to prevent this is nothing by comparison, and we must obviously spend more.

The plans to keep schools in these areas open year round is a step forward. Somehow I believe that the school is going to have to become the focus of activity in these areas. It can involve all the people in the neighborhood as no other institution can, and it is able to provide cultural enrichment for the people living there.

Assisting in Providing Food and Other Welfare Services

The Crime Prevention Bureau officer is better prepared than anyone else to know about human need in the ghetto. There are many public and private agencies working diligently to feed the needy, but they cannot always reach everybody or always be aware of who really needs assistance.

We learned that many people who were qualified to receive assistance, particularly with regard to the food surplus program, were seldom aware they qualified for such aid and furthermore had few means of finding out how to receive assistance.

We discovered that few residents of these areas have telephones and many could not operate one even if it were available. Again, it has become the policeman's job to seek a solution and clear away the roadblocks.

The question of city service is one of the most aggravating in the ghetto. The residents feel that the city government does not really care, for if the government cared their streets would be neatly paved, their garbage collected, the automobile wrecks towed away, etc., etc.

It had been the experience of the city government that whenever a slum area was cleared up it was in the same condition as before within a few weeks' time, and this often proved to be true. It was true in the past because there was generally no follow-up program. Now residents are encouraged to keep their neighborhoods clean and, with help from the city government, are doing so. The police stay behind those residents who tend to be chronic litterers and thus eliminate the cause. It is really rather simple. The residents know that the city cares because there is a police officer around every day checking. If the city cares—that vital someone else—then the residents of the ghetto begin to care and be more aware of their environment.

When someone in the area comes to the police with a request for some type of city service, such as garbage removal, the request is made by the citizen to the policeman on duty in the neighborhood and the policeman requests that the proper agency responsible for garbage removal, or whatever, get the job done. Since the policeman is in the area constantly he can check to see that the job is accomplished. If the job is not done, then the officer turns in a report to the department. If it concerns police functions, then the police take corrective action. If, on the other hand, it involves another facet of city government, such as garbage removal, then the report is forwarded to the Mayor's office where it is received by the Mayor's assistant, and ultimately by the Mayor himself, if necessary, for the proper action to be taken.

This system works only if you have a mayor and city administration dedicated to solving the problem demanding follow-up action from all city employees. Mayor Allen zealously made the operation a success in Atlanta. Without his determination to get things accomplished, reports would have just piled up and gathered dust in the usual bureaucratic way.

Providing Tough, Quick, and Reliable Police Service for the Residents of the Ghetto

The employment of Negro policemen many years before came about because of the high crime rate in Negro neighborhoods. Whatever the Negro has suffered from segregation and racism has been in part relieved in outbursts of violence by Negroes against one another. In spite of the rioting of later years, it is now and has been in the past the violence of Negroes against Negroes that remains the major police problem in all urban areas.

Properly trained Negro and white police officers working in the Crime Prevention Bureau can communicate with the people in these areas about the problem as no one else is able to do. If a Negro resident of the ghetto feels threatened he can express his fears to a Crime Prevention officer and the officer can investigate the situation and keep checking to see that the problem is solved.

In the beginning of the Crime Prevention program the residents of these high crime neighborhoods more readily confided their fears to a Negro officer than a white officer, since the distrust of all authority and the white police officer in particular was still strong in all of Atlanta's poor neighborhoods. Now the people in these areas appear more confident about the police and once the police have gained their confidence it doesn't matter what color a policeman is when he is needed. Our Crime Prevention officers are establishing contact with the community and building on it day by day. Of course you could never build this kind of confidence in these areas with the use of a segregated police force.

The biggest problem with police service in these areas is the traditional lack of follow-up. In years past persons would make complaints but, if the complaint did not seem too pressing to the authorities, the ghetto resident might never hear any more about what if anything was being done, and the person making the complaint might be severely beaten up or shot for "ratting" on his enemy.

The refusal of the conventional white police force to take the problems of the ghetto resident seriously is probably the major cause of rioting. For many years the police have been indifferent, although not always with malice or premeditation. Mostly the police were just too busy and too concerned with other matters to investigate fully.

Now when the police are in the ghetto for whatever reason, and whether an arrest is made or not, a copy of the report goes to Crime Prevention, which does a follow-up. Keeping in touch with the people is the most important aspect of crime prevention.

Acting as Advisers on Good Citizenship and Making Friends for the Atlanta Police Department

This is the political or, if you prefer, the public relations aspect of the program. The officers speak about crime prevention to many adult groups such as the PTAs, civic organizations, and schools both in and out of poor neighborhoods. They talk earnestly on the subject of respect for city, state, and federal laws. They talk about respect for authority in the home. The Crime Prevention officer is expected to get involved in a variety of activities for young people.

Atlanta also has organized the junior deputy and junior crime prevention clubs. These two groups on the elementary school level include such activities as sightseeing tours of the police station, firehouses, waterworks, and other operations of the city government and projects promoting interest and involvement in crime prevention work. Vehicles used by the Crime Prevention Bureau officers have special equipment such as loudspeakers, record players, and sprinkler heads. They can close off streets to vehicular traffic and hold street meetings with some entertainment; as many as 2,500 kids in one area have participated at a single time in the SKATE-O-RAMA contests, a very popular roller-skating event during the winter months. In hot weather they hook up sprinkler heads to fire hydrants. One of the major riots to occur in any American city was begun when the police turned off fire hydrants that kids had opened on a sweltering summer day.

On many occasions the Crime Prevention officers have had all the children from a housing project playing under the sprinkler in one block.

Various complaints are handled by Crime Prevention officers, including malicious mischief, petty larceny, missing persons, stolen bicycles, and nearly all juvenile cases.

Malicious Mischief. The ghetto youngsters must live on the streets and consequently do a lot of standing around on street corners. Because white middle-class youngsters do not have to do this, the police have always assumed that the ghetto youngster was simply a troublemaker. The thinking was that only hoodlums stood around on street corners.

Until a few years ago every police officer in the country would have insisted that this was the case. Nowadays we must look deeper. Youngsters cluster on street corners because there is very often no place else to go, not because they are hoodlums. However, standing around on street corners with nothing to do is an invitation for trouble and in such a situation malicious mischief can quickly lead to something far more serious. It is Crime Prevention's responsibility to provide activities like those we have mentioned to give the ghetto youngster something to do with his time.

Petty Larceny. This is a big problem, but again is nearly always a case of residents of the slum stealing from each other. Suppose someone has a transistor radio stolen from his home. The owner calls the police, handling the case in the traditional manner. When the police arrive the owner tells them that he believes that one John Doe has taken his radio. The police go and arrest John Doe, recover the radio, and the entangled bureaucratic legal process is cranked up, often prolonged over several months. All over a stolen radio. Under the Crime Prevention Bureau system the officer goes and finds John Doe (since the officer works the area daily, he probably knows John Doe, what kind of person he is, where he works, if he has a police record, etc.), and if it is strictly a case of petty larceny the CP officer most likely can persuade John Doe to return the radio. Without making an arrest, the CP officer will stress individual pride and community pride in an attempt to prevent this minor offense from leading to something more serious in the future.

Missing Persons. There is a certain vagabond quality to life in most ghettos. Roaming around is one of the few free pleasures. The adults do it and the children soon learn to do it too. Sometimes a very young ghetto youngster may wander off and be gone several days without a missing persons report being made. And, again, the same kid may wander off for the night and the people responsible for him may be hysterical in their worry about where he might be or if anything has happened to him. Here CP provides a great service. The CP officers know the habits and habitats of the residents and can usually round up an errant youngster on short notice. The complicated procedure of making out formal missing person reports and the red tape that goes with it are completely eliminated.

Stolen Bicycles. Remember the childhood incident that Muhammad Ali described in his autobiography and what the police officer told him when his bicycle was stolen? The officer told him that he would have to learn to fight if he didn't want some other underprivileged kid to steal his bike. With the aid of the police Muhammad Ali learned to fight— but what of the other children of the poor neighborhoods who do not have such a talent?

The point is that as an adult the one incident in his childhood that made a big impression on Muhammad Ali was when his bicycle was stolen. It was his most prized possession, the only object that gave him status as an individual; then it was stolen. At that moment this Negro boy knew what it was to be a poor resident of a high crime neighborhood.

86

How many other boys in similar situations have the lesson brought home to them in the same way?

"I live in a world where nobody cares. There is no law, no justice. I wanted this bicycle all my life and now that I have gotten it, someone steals it from me. The world is against me. Society is rotten. People take things away from you and the cops do nothing. When I get older I am going to take things too. This is the system."

Except that when the ghetto kid gets older it will be bigger things than bicycles.

Kids. Bicycles. The Crime Prevention Bureau officer. Seemingly not very important elements in the fight against crime—until you stop and think it over. But they are mighty important and will be even more important in the years ahead.

The CP officer's job is to find solutions to all the problems that arise daily in slum neighborhoods if possible, without making an arrest. We have tried to adopt a page from the Juvenile Court's manual by making the Crime Prevention Bureau a correctional organization rather than a punitive one. The CP Bureau officers have earned the respect of most of the people living in their districts. They have also earned the respect of other members of the department, and we have had requests from other officers of the department to be transferred to the CP Bureau.

Patrolling police officers on regular duty assignments are quick to call CP for assistance when they see problems developing and we believe that everyone in the department now believes that we are moving in the right direction. We expect to see the CP Bureau grow and expand and this will certainly call for the expenditure of more money. In its first year (1966) the CP Bureau grew to twenty-nine in police personnel and included within this group a captain and three lieutenants.

The CP Bureau officers must always wear two hats; when they find an individual or group that cannot be persuaded by their aid and counseling to obey the law, they must then arrest these individuals and prosecute them, for the highest value of the law remains in the keeping of the peace whether by new or traditional means.

Concurrent with the creation and expansion of the CP Bureau within the Atlanta Police Department has come the organization of a special Task Force of about thirty specially trained and equipped officers, who can be moved into any community on short notice, to use whatever force is necessary to enforce the law and maintain the peace. These officers have special training in the tactics of crowd control and are familiar with ghetto neighborhoods and the problems the police will encounter there in periods of turmoil.

We are convinced that the action of the CP Bureau has prevented the crime record from rising as rapidly as it would have had we not had the CP Bureau. We are also convinced that when street disturbances do occur the CP Bureau's actions keep them from being as severe as they might have been otherwise.

Street fighting or riots, as they have come to be called, erupted in Atlanta in September of 1966. Two detectives were in a slum neighborhood attempting to arrest a man for automobile larceny, and the man was shot when he tried to flee from the detectives. This caused a large crowd to gather in the streets. They were in an angry mood.

Mayor Allen appeared immediately on the scene and elbowed his way to the center of the crowd. He did a great job in confronting the group face to face, attempting to quiet the crowd. He would have succeeded except that SNCC was on the scene too and incited the crowd to start throwing bricks and bottles at the Mayor and the police. The Mayor was addressing the group from atop an automobile and the angry mob began rocking the car. The Mayor had to leap for his life —barely escaping serious injury.

The police then moved into the area in force and cleared the streets with the use of tear gas. It was necessary to seal off the area, call in off-duty policemen and place the department on twelve-hour-per-day duty. Seventy-three persons were arrested in this incident, several of whom were indicted by the grand jury for inciting to riot.

Five days later a white motorist, driving through another Negro community in a different section of town, shot and killed a Negro youth. Again an angry mob gathered in the street and again Mayor Allen moved right into their midst to urge peace and a return to order. This was a great example of how a modern American mayor must deal with such a crisis, and he succeeded in persuading many of the people in the streets to return to their homes. Some in the group were violent and angry and refused to disperse. They shouted threats and insults and started throwing bricks and bottles. Ten store windows were broken and several buildings were set afire, but the police were there in force. The fires were promptly extinguished and there was no looting. The streets were cleared and sixty-five persons were arrested on the first night, fourteen adults and fifteen juveniles arrested as the disorder continued into the second night. Afterwards there was no more disturbance. The quick apprehension by the police of the white man who shot the Negro boy helped cool down the situation. The individual was ultimately tried and convicted and given life for murder. In December of 1967 the individual won a new trial and this time pleaded guilty to manslaughter and received a twenty-year sentence.

We in the Police Department felt at the time and still feel that the best way for the police to handle a situation after it has reached this point is for them to speak politely, move about very slowly and deliberately and begin taking into custody those who are ringleaders in the disturbance. Of course, the best solution is not to allow the situation to reach this point if at all possible.

The city of Atlanta did not wait until there were street disturbances to improve living conditions in the low-income communities. The city, in cooperation with the federal government and private industry, is responsible for the existence of several low-income housing projects. At the urging of city government, local businesses were involved in retraining programs and attempting to employ the hard core unemployed long before it became fashionable. In every way that it could, city government took the lead in the decade of the sixties in attempting to assist the people living in poverty communities.

The Police Department's role in all of this was primarily the creation of the Crime Prevention Bureau. We in the department were convinced that the disorders of 1966 were much less severe because of the work done by the CP Bureau and we were sure that the continued peace and tranquillity of the city depended on the enlargement and development of this group.

6

Street Fighting,
Civil Disorders, and Riots

The year 1967 saw crime and civil disorders escalating at an alarming rate throughout the nation. On June 19 of that year a private uniformed guard for a merchant in the Dixie Hills section of Atlanta attempted to arrest a young boy for larceny. The boy's sister interfered and they both resisted. When the police were called to assist the guard a crowd gathered and started throwing bricks and bottles. As more police arrived the barrage intensified, injuring several police officers. The police returned the fire and one Negro man was killed and three other Negroes were injured. Following two nights of disturbances thirty-three persons were arrested. Mayor Allen issued an emergency proclamation placing a curfew on the community but it never became necessary to enforce it.

The Crime Prevention Bureau began patrolling the area, assuring the residents that every complaint would be investigated and acted upon. Negro leaders went into the area urging calm. There was no third night of disturbance.

The Dixie Hills section is not a slum. It is a comparatively new housing project with good streets, good recreational equipment, and good apartment houses occupied by middle-class Negroes.

Three weeks after the incident 200 residents appeared before the regular meeting of the Police Committee for a complete airing of the Dixie Hills matter. The Police Committee consists of five members from the Aldermanic Board (which is like a city council) which oversees the work of the Police Department. After the Police Committee ran hurriedly through its regular agenda it listened to some five hours of testimony from the residents of Dixie Hills.

One witness stated that the real problem in Dixie Hills was the fact that many of the residents were moving farther out in the suburbs, leaving their apartments to be occupied by families from slum communities who were not so orderly as the former residents. It seemed that both white and Negro police tended to judge the entire section by this lowest common denominator.

The committee assured the residents that their complaints would be given every consideration and I suggested that they help me find two men in their community qualified for jobs in the Police Department who would be assigned to patrol their neighborhood. They responded readily to the suggestion and it was ultimately implemented.

In July a young Negro man walked into a shirt shop in downtown Atlanta and got involved in a dispute with the white woman manager over the use of the restroom. The woman denied that the restroom was for use of customers in the store. The Negro man insisted that white customers used it and that it was simply not available to Negroes. The argument became intense and the Negro man walked out of the store, picked up a brick, and heaved it through the plate-glass window.

SNCC leaders gathered at the scene, were indeed present when the fracas began, and quite a few rocks and bottles were thrown inflicting minor injuries on several police. Nine persons were arrested, the store manager was escorted from the store, and no further trouble developed from this incident. Three days later Mayor Allen stated in very clear and firm language the goals, the policies, and the responsibilities of the city of Atlanta and the Atlanta Police Department. It was an excellent statement and I repeat the gist of it here.

"The city of Atlanta will not slow down in providing equal services for all its citizens. There are opportunities for dissent ... and demonstrations by dissatisfied citizens ... the city welcomes this, but they must be conducted within the confines of the law ... and there can be no exceptions. The city will not be intimidated by the threat of violence, and lawlessness will not be tolerated. The burning and looting of property will not be tolerated. There will be no hesitancy whatsoever to use the necessary means to enforce law and order in a law-abiding community ... the Atlanta Police have been trained to avoid what has been termed police brutality ... and to provide equal protection and service for all citizens and all visitors. The police have the authority, under the law, to protect themselves while enforcing the law. The police will not be subjected to being shot at, having bottles and bricks thrown at them, without taking appropriate action. The Atlanta Police Department has furnished a very fine service and they have operated under great restraint.... The Atlanta police do not push anyone around, nor will they be pushed around, and will not hesitate to request the assistance of the National Guard if events indicate it is necessary to provide the protection and services that law-abiding citizens of our city have every right to expect."

We got through the remainder of the summer without any more disturbances. This was due largely to the efforts of the CP Bureau. During this summer 52 American cities suffered civil disorders, street fighting, and riots that caused many deaths and injuries to the population and the police of those cities. Looting and burning were responsible for property damage costing many millions of dollars. The local police in most of those cities kept the situation under reasonable control and held property damage to a minimum, but there were many arrests and some deaths and injuries in all of them. In some cases it was necessary to call on the state police and the National Guard to restore order, and in one city it was necessary to call on the U.S. Army to restore order.

On July 27 President Johnson, by executive order, appointed a National Advisory Commission on Civil Disorders. The previous evening the President had gone on television to address the American people and announced the formation of a "Riot Commission." Attorney General Ramsey Clark called and told me of the President's plans for the commission. He told me that the President wanted me to serve and he asked me if I would do so.

The commission was headed by Governor Otto Kerner, who was appointed chairman, while Mayor John Lindsay was made vice-chairman and David Ginsburg acted as executive director. The other members included Senators Fred Harris and Edward Brooke; Congressmen James C. Corman and William M. McCulloch; I. W. Abel, Charles B. Thornton, Roy Wilkins, and Katherine Graham Peden.

I was deeply grateful for the opportunity to serve on such a distinguished commission and it was the greatest challenge ever to come my way. I think also that I was appointed because the city of Atlanta had been trying for the past twenty years to solve the race problem.

The commission held its first meeting in the Indian Treaty

room of the old State, War, and Navy Building in Washington on the night following its being empaneled by President Johnson. The country had suffered much from civil disorders and it was our main concern to do what we could to put an end to them.

We met two days a week in Washington throughout the fall and winter of 1967-68. We visited several of the cities that had suffered the greatest damage from disturbances. The full Commission questioned more than a hundred witnesses, including governors, mayors, chiefs of police, rioters, professors, and everyone else concerned with civil disorders. The commission sat for seven months and finished its report on March 1, 1968. The rest is history. Although there was much division within the commission during its investigations, the report was unanimously adopted and signed by all the members.

During our discussions one member of the commission raised the point that he doubted there was any correlation between poverty and rioting. I insisted that early in their police experience policemen learn that there is a definite relationship between the two. An incident in a middle-class neighborhood can be handled by a lone police officer as a matter of routine without disturbing the community. In a poor neighborhood, however, a lone policeman can sometimes do the same, but often crowds gather quickly (the streets of the ghetto are nearly always filled with people) and a disorder can be set off almost by osmosis. This is a characteristic of the ghetto. Regarding the police as a kind of foreign power is also a characteristic of the ghetto. The presence of police in the ghetto causes the residents to feel threatened much as though the police were an invading army.

Most questions that came before the commission were discussed at length and their inclusion in the report was then decided by majority vote. One subject that never got anywhere was that of sex. Several members of the staff felt that something on this subject should have been included in the report and that the commission should have made some sort of study of the relationship between racism and sexual attitudes. When asked for my opinion I said that I thought sex had always been at the root of the racial problem in the South. After a long silence the commission moved on to other matters and the subject was not brought up again.

All the members of the Atlanta Police Department were required to read the riot report and file a paper on what they had read. Some of the reports made interesting reading and occasionally made unusual reading. Confident, no doubt, that the reports would be read by their superior officers, several policemen wrote thorough summaries but included in their report some mild complaints. Several complained that an arbitrary day for changeover from winter to summer uniforms was not realistic in a city with an unpredictable climate and a police force that worked men twenty-four hours a day—the day watch in summer uniform weather, the morning watch still needing to be winterized. The department eventually issued an order making summer uniforms optional throughout the year and leaving it up to the officers themselves to use their own best judgment in such matters.

One of the things recommended by both the Atlanta Crime Commission and the President's Commission on Civil Disorders was the employment of Community Service officers by urban police departments. The Kerner Commission recommended that the federal government should pay up to 90 percent of the costs of employment of CS officers by police departments which met certain requirements of personnel and procedures. In spite of this recommendation and the fact that it was summer again, there was no action from national or state governments.

Mayor Allen, however, on his own initiative, made money

available for the city of Atlanta to hire 50 Community Service officers, the first to be employed in the nation. These young men were individuals living in the ghetto who were largely without training and jobs. They were issued uniforms but no weapons. It was their job to help keep their neighborhoods "cool" through the long hot summers.

The CP Bureau is now a separate unit of the Police Department and is no longer under the wing of the detective division. It has been moved into new quarters opening directly onto the street. This makes the office convenient to walk-in traffic and utilizes the "store-front" concept.

The bureau consists of about fifty officers under the command of Superintendent Oscar Jordan, who is white, while the special Task Force of about forty officers is under the command of Captain Howard Baugh, a Negro. Task Force officers are specially trained in riot control and have had extensive investigative experience and possess a sure knowledge of the ghetto. Although the number will vary, this unit usually consists of about two thirds Negro officers and one third white officers. The officers of the Task Force have had extensive experience in CP. They normally patrol in high crime areas on the evening watch; however, in times of unrest they can work any hours for they are a special unit and are not included in the total number of men allotted to the evening watch.

Each Crime Prevention Bureau officer has a number of the CSO's working under him to assist in carrying out his duties and in organizing activities within the neighborhood. These officers also work with private groups such as the Jaycees, who have an extensive program going in poor neighborhoods.

In most cases the reason the CSO's were recruited by the CP Bureau is that they had been involved with the police over some minor violation of the law. By making such a person a CSO, it is hoped this responsibility will curb his unlawful instincts and orient him toward more useful endeavors within an orderly society. Persons with more serious violations of the law on their records cannot be included in this group. Some of the CSO's when they reach the qualifying age hopefully will become police officers, and we think we have found a way not only to cool off high crime areas but recruit police officers too.

Superintendent Jordan also runs a training school within the CP Bureau. All new men hired by the Atlanta Police Department will now work in CP before their regular training and before going into any other division of the department. We are doing this to acquaint the new police officer with the problem at the very outset of his career. It gives the department a chance to size up the man in a situation in which he will often find himself. If the man shows no understanding of this aspect of police procedure we don't want him, and it is far better at the beginning to try to eliminate any future cause of a major riot. Most major civil disorders in the United States have been caused by unwise and/or hasty police action. This tendency to thoughtless action within all police departments must be eliminated and we in Atlanta feel that the best time to work against it is in the beginning.

The primary purpose of CP is to do what its name implies. How is it doing? In the crucial area of civil disorders, quite well. The CP Bureau also has the backing of the Police Department. Officers who once scoffed at CP have asked to be assigned to that division. Ultimately we hope that it will no longer be necessary to maintain CP as a separate unit, and that every police officer in the department can be a policeman wearing two hats: one for police service and one for social service. Until that day comes we will continue to enlarge and beef up the CP Bureau. Hopefully state or federal funds will one day be available to help do the job.

One problem no one has successfully dealt with, including CP Bureaus, regular police procedures, press, etc., is the rise in homicides by firearms in the nation. All thoughtful people have been appalled by the figures and the country has been severely shaken by the growing list of national figures who have been gunned to death in recent years. It is a problem afflicting every city and every community.

The gun which is purchased on the spur of the moment in a time of hysteria may be kept at home, and after a time may be forgotten. Until a child comes upon it and shoots himself or a playmate or until a husband or wife decides to settle an intense domestic squabble by resorting to firearms. People are being killed every day in their own homes with their own guns which they originally purchased to protect themselves from some vague menace. Most guns fired in industrial robberies were stolen by criminals at a previous residential break-in. And remember, the most dangerous item in any household is a gun.

I believe any attempt to prohibit the selling of guns would be about as successful as was the attempt in the twenties to prohibit the sale of alcoholic beverages. But the sale of firearms *can* be controlled. All firearms in private hands should be registered. This should be done on the federal level so that we would have a uniform standard throughout the country. The buyer of a firearm should also be required to purchase a license and keep that license updated on a yearly basis. The police should have the authority to confiscate all illegal firearms and destroy them.

The impetus that has caused the white middle class to supply itself with guns has been the rise in crime and civil disorders. When the civil rights movement abandoned its completely nonviolent approach, much of the white middle class in the country was shocked and frightened, and went on a gun-buying spree. The motive of those groups who aban-

99

doned nonviolence was to achieve their goals through fear and intimidation. It was designed for shock treatment for a complacent America; and was rather effective, if the large number of firearms sold can be cited as an indication.

Fortunately for society, most of the Negro population has completely rejected violence as a means of solving social problems and has adopted a wait-and-see attitude, hoping for progress through traditional democratic means. A majority of the white and Negro population recognizes that change must come to our lives, and must come about peaceably.

The motives behind those advocates of violence within our society are nearly identical to the motives behind the now-defunct Ku Klux Klan. We endured the Klan for fifty years and can endure those advocates of violence of today for just as long as necessary. Ultimately separatism based on race simply will not work. Among other things, it always leads, even without intending to do so, to the worst kind of violence. The nation will tolerate this for just so long.

The white population and most of the Negro population have been frightened by civil disorders, assassinations, and rioting, and they are looking to the police to stop it now. I believe that the police have the best public support today that we have ever had during all the country's history. But this wide public support must not push us into excesses and court baiting—and if white public pressure often demands an eye for an eye and a tooth for a tooth, the local police must be prepared to make the preservation of law, order, and justice for all the first order of business.

The highest value of the law is in the keeping of the peace. The mayor and the chief of police in any city have sole responsibility to protect life and property in the community and to maintain law and order in their respective jurisdictions. Every city must have the necessary equipment and trained personnel to solve these problems and, if a street

100

disorder does occur, to move in immediately with sufficient force to stop it before it gets out of control. If they cannot do this, the mayor has the responsibility to ask the governor to furnish National Guard protection. If this is insufficient, the governor has the responsibility to ask the President of the United States to order the U.S. Army to come in and restore order, or even to prevent civil disorders.

The President has found it necessary to take such action eighteen times in the past 175 years. President Eisenhower sent troops into Little Rock, Arkansas, in 1957 and President Johnson ordered federal troops into Detroit, Washington, D.C., Baltimore, and Chicago in the years 1967 and 1968. These are important eventualities that must be considered in all police training and police planning in the future.

The only real way to control a riot is to prevent it. We have seen repeatedly that the National Guard or the army cannot prevent a riot—they can stop it for sure but they are not given the training nor the equipment nor the day-to-day contact with the community necessary to prevent disorders. If civil disorders and rioting are to be prevented they must be prevented by local communities and local police. Presidents Eisenhower, Kennedy, Johnson, and Nixon have made it very clear that this is a local and state responsibility and they never interfered unless there was a breakdown and failure at the local and state levels.

Here in Atlanta a retired U.S. brigadier general is director of Atlanta's Civil Defense; in accordance with instructions from the mayor, he and the adjutant general of Georgia have drawn up an excellent plan to coordinate the action of the police and the National Guard if it ever becomes necessary or desirable for the city of Atlanta to request the assistance of the National Guard. The National Guard units that would be called up in case of an emergency have had very special training, and they have been instructed that riot control is

101

not the same thing as ordinary combat. In ordinary combat everyone out in front of you is your deadly enemy, and you shoot everything that moves. In riot control everyone out in front of you is *not* your enemy, and in fact most of the time is a fellow officer.

The problem of looting has been widely and loudly discussed. Should looters be treated as the enemy and shot? Not if there is an adequate, well-trained riot police in the area, for in that case there will be no looting. The attempt by a few policemen to control massive looting in a widespread disorder by shooting looters could very easily turn into a street massacre in which innocent citizens might be injured or killed. The great debate on whether or not to shoot looters misses the point, for if and when this stage is reached local police procedure is pretty much of a failure. The only solution lies in preventing the situation from reaching this point. The police are charged with this duty and responsibility and they must meet it.

The Atlanta Police Department has continued to strengthen and expand its program in keeping with fast-moving events. Part of the difficulty is that a course of action proper to one season is not necessarily a proper course of action for the next. In any emergency we cancel all leaves and days off and all members of the department go onto 12-hour shifts, seven days a week. This procedure alone more than doubles the police personnel available for street duty. At these times police officers work 84 hours per week, instead of 40 hours. Every officer below the rank of captain receives time and a half overtime pay. This means that the number of officers assigned to the trouble area may equal the total number of police personnel ordinarily assigned to patrol duty, leaving an equal number of officers to patrol the parts of the city not involved in the disorder.

A city ordinance authorizes the mayor to define the boundaries and identify the area where civil disorders are occurring or expected to occur and to request the assistance of the National Guard when needed. The mayor has the full authority and responsibility to make this determination. When the Guard arrives on the scene police officers are to be assigned to accompany them on their mission. The police will take into custody and detain all persons who should be arrested. The police will process and present all prisoners and witnesses to the courts and the Guard will deliver any injured persons to the medical center. Additional action by the police or the Guard will be subject to orders issued on the scene by the adjutant general or his subordinate officer.

It was the unanimous conclusion of the Atlanta Commission on Crime and Juvenile Delinquency, the President's Commission on Law Enforcement and Administration of Justice, and the National Advisory Commission on Civil Disorders that poverty, crime, and civil unrest are so closely intertwined that to speak of one without the other is to falsify the issue. J. Edgar Hoover has testified that the FBI failed to discover any evidence of conspiracy in the civil disorders occurring through 1967. We must look elsewhere for the causes.

The police have been accused of aggravating and in some cases causing riots by their intemperate response in tense situations. I believe the police must bear a part of the blame. But it is still true to say that there are no secret weapons available for reducing crime or preventing riots. Part of the answer undoubtedly lies in assuming that the police act with good judgment and with measured actions taken responsibly. But until the whole problem is attacked—on a national scale —and its root causes dealt with we will not see the end of turmoil in our cities. Federal programs in housing, education, employment, and firearms control must be supported and pushed on all levels of government, with federal, state, and

103

local governments all working together to treat the conditions which have brought us to this pass.

Atlanta has officially supported all federal programs designed to meet the crisis and under the strong leadership of Mayor Allen has gone a long way toward meeting its responsibilities. As Mayor Allen puts it, "We cannot afford to wait for discontent to disrupt into disorder before we take action" and "we shall never permit disorder but we shall always make every effort to eliminate the basic conditions and abuses that build up the pressures which explode into disorder."

The importance of having mayors with the understanding and foresight of a Mayor Allen was brought to the test and proved to the nation and the world the night Dr. Martin Luther King was assassinated. It was Mayor Allen who sped to Mrs. King's side and assisted her in making plans to fly to Memphis even before word reached them that Dr. King was dead. It was as though the Atlanta Police Department had spent the past twenty years preparing for that unforgettable week in April of 1968.

We were holding a meeting at police headquarters discussing police matters and plans for the approaching summer months when word came that Dr. King had been shot in Memphis. We immediately dispatched police to the King residence and to the residence of Dr. King's parents and kept the police there day and night. It was an attempt to provide the family with whatever assistance was needed.

My own last communication from Dr. King was a telegram I had received a few weeks prior to his assassination. I include it here only because I cherish it.

"You, as a member of the President's Commission on Civil Disorders, deserve the gratitude of the nation because you had both the wisdom to perceive the truth and the courage to state it. The commission's findings that America is a racist

104

society and that white racism is the root cause of today's urban disorders is an important confession of a harsh truth. My only hope is that white America and our national government will heed your warnings and implement your recommendations. By ignoring them we will sink inevitably into a nightmarish doomsday. God grant that your excellent report will educate the nation and lead to action before it is too late."

When we got word that rioting and vandalism had broken out in several major cities we immediately put into effect our emergency plan and placed all members of the force on 12-hour shifts. The CP Bureau offered assistance to groups that began going through the neighborhoods urging the people not to resort to violence. Meetings were quickly called by such groups as the "Pittsburg Teen Town."

The Pittsburg group drafted a statement which read in part: "There will be riots. We will become a target for people up to no good" ... "People, please think before you act. Try to reason out your actions before you commit yourselves," and this is exactly what they did. Plans for action were formulated and within hours volunteers were moving about the neighborhoods urging calm. Police provided transportation and other assistance. We decided early that in a situation of this magnitude there was no rule book to go by. We simply played it by ear and tried to keep in the background as much as possible. The key word in the department during this week was "flexibility."

Mayor Allen set the tone for the city and the police by his attitude of sincere regret at the death of Dr. King. Everyone knew that his regret was genuine because Mayor Allen was a friend and admirer of Dr. King. His grief and sympathy for the family were not an act.

The city of Atlanta had given Dr. King a dinner following his receiving of the Nobel Peace Prize. Mayor Allen had presided at the dinner and my wife and I, along with two other members of the department and their wives, had attended along with hundreds of other Atlantans.

Dr. King's father had been well known in Atlanta for many years and was well known by many members of the Police Department. Because of this background a rather remarkable understanding of the situation swept through the department and an awareness that the Negro people had lost a great leader quickly became the sentiment of all the police personnel. We determined to do everything we could to mourn with them.

With the exception of activating our previous plan of placing everyone in the department on a 12-hour shift, no special orders or directives were issued. I had complete confidence in the superior officers in the department and felt that if they did not know by now what to do all the memos and directives in the world were much too late. The superior officers all felt the same way about the men under their command. Police officers working together simply resolved that there would be no trouble in their districts.

On Hunter Street the night before the funeral several Negro youths broke a window of a liquor store and carried away some bottles. A few CP Bureau officers quietly investigated the theft and there was very little noise or commotion. No crowds gathered. A city was not lost. There was no looting or burning. The effectiveness of police training can only be measured by performance. The performance the Atlanta police turned in during this week in April, 1968, convinced me that our training, begun some twenty years before, was indeed effective.

On the day of Dr. King's funeral we held the morning watch over and pulled in the evening watch early. For the first and only time in our history every man in the Atlanta Police Department was working at the same time.

106

Rain had been forecast but did not materialize. The day of the funeral was cloudy—and hot. By daylight the police traffic division had the area in front of Ebenezer Baptist Church roped off. There were thousands of people in town for the funeral and many spent the night in white and Negro churches. Thousands more slept on the ground in a vacant lot directly across from the church. About an hour before the funeral the crush of people broke through the police ropes and literally engulfed the area in front of the church in a sea of humanity.

With a good deal of firmness and shoving the police could have pushed the people back and cleared the street, but had they done so there was the possibility of creating an unpleasant incident and this was not the time or place for that. Instead, the police joined hands with the SCLC staffers and cleared an aisle for the notables to enter the church. Many could not get inside. Approximately fifty representatives and United States senators and other dignitaries stood in the street and listened to the funeral over transistor radios.

No unpleasant incident marred Dr. King's funeral. A city the size of Atlanta was not accustomed to the influx of people that arrived and the crowds that formed for the funeral, but we handled it as best we could.

What I am trying to stress here is the vital importance of attitude. The most important thing in relationships between people is the attitude they harbor toward each other. The essential core of police training, beyond instilling professionalism into the individual, should be the creation of an enlightened and proper attitude toward others. In the society in which we live a proper attitude is also a central aspect of professionalism. No matter how well an individual is trained in other areas, he is of little value as a police officer if he is a bigot. But for changes in attitude to take place on the level of the patrolman, the men who command the department must take responsibility. In Atlanta we have stressed to the men in our department that they must be color-blind; and it makes no difference what minority group is referred to.

There are those who say that the police in America are rapidly becoming a group not identifiable with any social class within our society. I think this is only partly true. I also think that such a development is not all bad. For too long the police, particularly in Southern communities, have been an arm of the Ku Klux Klan and the White Citizens' Council, enforcing these groups' ideas of right and wrong. In the cities many big police departments have long been the domain of one cultural, ethnic group whose ideas and codes of behavior have become entrenched as police policy.

It is the responsibility of the police to enforce the law, not support a cultural bias. A man may not be regarded as criminal simply because he has no job. Nor can he be regarded as a criminal simply because he lives in a high crime neighborhood. Nor should a man be regarded as a criminal simply because he stands around on street corners, has long hair or a beard, wears unusual clothes, and is not a "real" American. The police must be on guard against shifts in the public's attitudes too, looking not to public opinion but to the law as the final arbitrator of their behavior.

For example, in September of 1962 I was invited to speak at the University of California on the subject of "The Police and Cultural Tensions." The police officials and school people were most cordial and friendly and all the talk was very liberal, socially concerned, and focused on how we must help the disadvantaged within our society. In April of 1964 I went again to California for a speech, but this time found the atmosphere entirely changed. Now the mood among the police personnel and professional and academic people was that we had been tolerant long enough but that we could be tolerant no longer. Law and order above all. This was my first experience with the so-called "backlash" sentiment.

It has been said that California is a microcosm of the rest of the country and in this case it seems to be true. For years the white liberal has fought for gains for the Negroes. But when what he has been fighting for has suddenly become a reality in the sixties, there has been a shift of emphasis from moving ahead for further gains to consolidate at the point reached. The liberal goes along with the agitation for Negro rights until there is some leader who goes too far in his eyes. Then there is a reaction, usually followed by some gross excess on the part of the establishment, which in turn creates a new wave of sentiment for the oppressed. This is what President Kennedy had in mind when he reportedly said that Bull Connor's police dogs had done more than anything else for the cause of civil rights in that period. The police should retain their composure no matter what the prevailing public feelings are and seek to assure the protection of the law for everyone.

There has been rioting—by Negroes, by college students, and by those opposed to the Vietnam War. In the case of rioting by Negroes, in no city has rioting occurred more than once in a specific locality. Why is this?

In the first place, rioting hurts the people who live in the slum areas more than it hurts anyone else. They are burned out of their homes. The business establishments where many of the people are employed also are destroyed. Business is scared away from the area by disorder and high insurance rates or the threat of no insurance, which reduces the number of jobs in areas where the job market is already tight.

In the second place, rioting brings results. The police change their practices and give more time and attention to good police service in the ghetto. They stop using thoughtless language with the residents because they are afraid it may lead to a bad incident. The fear of causing a riot has had the effect of leading to better police methods and better police service.

Service by welfare agencies too is improved after rioting, as they cut out the red tape and get aid and assistance to the people in riot areas. Private business and service organizations get involved in the life of the ghetto. They set up training programs and make jobs available for the residents. In short, up to a point rioting brings results.

The mainly white middle class is terrified that the looting and burning will come their way if they do not bestir themselves sufficiently to make things better for the have-nots. And it *will* come their way if white society grows complacent once again after the rioting has subsided. To my way of thinking this will not occur because I believe, as Dr. King said, we have a new day, a firmer will in America at present. However, those cities that do nothing had better beware. The devastation we have seen once can come again if we are not "involved."

All of which leads to a fuller discussion of a deeper problem. How does society maintain law and order with justice? To a large degree, in our society it is the job of the police and the judicial system to maintain law and order. What means are available to do this? Since the dawn of civilization the means by which individuals have been persuaded to obey the law has been the threat and severity of punishment.

The fact that the threat and the severity of punishment is not only a major part but an essential factor in getting people to obey the law, and therefore is standard police practice, will no doubt come as a shock to many people. For centuries of Western history specific offenses were punished by certain death. People once were put to death for what now could only be considered minor crimes or petty offenses. In the twentieth century society has largely come around to the point of view that capital punishment not only does not

110

reduce crime but is a barbaric means for a civilized society to employ for whatever end and should be done away with. The trend in most Western countries is to prohibit capital punishment. But what should the proper use of punishment be in reference to crime? Of course, crimes vary in degree of harmfulness and justification and the penalties applied must also be tempered to suit the crime. On the other hand, society's agent—the police—should not be deprived of the weapons necessary to deal with law violators, even if the severity of punishment is lessened as time goes by.

I have for many years continued to favor the use of capital punishment. In the opinion of many people this position has been thought inconsistent with my liberal view in other matters. In theory it may be inconsistent but in practice it is not. For, remember, it is the policeman's lot to put things into practice; he is generally not a theorist. It has always been my conviction that certainty of punishment, if not a deterrent to crime, does possibly contain the unlawful act. If society determines to abandon capital punishment, or punishment in general, as a means of controlling crime, then society must come forward with alternative means for control. Inadequate a means as it is for controlling crime, capital punishment is still a method of some efficacy and other methods are going to have to be devised now that it has been all but abandoned in our society.

In a similar way, when the police are charged with controlling a student confrontation, a civil rights march, or a picket line of striking workers, they must be trained for the job, employing modern techniques of control and not resorting to club-swinging retaliation. This means that the police must develop revolutionary, positive, helpful ways and techniques for dealing with people. Up to now we have seen but the modest beginnings of such training and education.

We have operated this way in the past because we have

111

always lacked the education, the training, and the funds to operate in any other manner. Granted that the entire emphasis in police management in the past twenty years has been to try to get away from the use of intimidation and force, I would be less than honest if I did not say it is still an important part of police procedure. I would also be derelict in my duty if I did not say that it is going to have to be replaced by some better procedures. The survival of the country depends upon it. The problem is that everyone is afraid to take the first step. Of course the first step has to be crime prevention—but it will require many more steps in the future.

In Atlanta, after we had the CP Bureau for two years, we were hit by the backlash. Cities such as San Francisco and Miami had similar experiences. We had discovered that creation of a CP Bureau has immediate and direct effects on crime in the ghetto. The incidence of crime immediately dropped by some 20 percent after the implementation of a CP Bureau. This is all to the good. Everyone was pleased and delighted with the program's success. The hard-liners who said it was a lot of nonsense were amazed, and were silenced for a time.

But after the first two years the *over-all* crime rate in the community began to go wildly upward. The doubting Thomases began to say, "We told you so! The only way to have law and order is by the use of a little force and head cracking." It seemed not enough to be tough and tolerant. In Miami, after two years of CP, the department abolished its community involvement program and adopted a hard-nosed hard-line policy that drew applause and support from all over the nation. But I do not think we can return to the old ways; it would be courting disaster to attempt to do so. We must work effectively in both crime prevention and law enforcement. We must render social services among the poor as well as continue tough police service.

112

Many abuses of civil liberties and civil rights have been allowed to continue up to recent times. It is in the light of such abuses that we must look at the Supreme Court's rulings on proper police procedures.

In the past segregation in the South was not designed to keep the Negro separate but to keep him down. As the government arm in carrying out the policy of segregation, the police did their part in keeping the Negro in his place. Under legal segregation the Negro had no rights, and so the police did not have to be careful about violating them! When crime got out of hand the police could swoop into an area and arrest everyone there for no apparent reason. Standard police practice was to hold periodic raids on "bad" places and hangouts of "known criminals." These raids would bring in innocent and guilty alike and would frighten and intimidate everyone in the area. The word would go out that the cops were on the rampage so everyone had better cool it for a while.

For both innocent and guilty thirty or sixty days in the work camp was thought an excellent crime preventive and in fact for a while there would be little crime in that particular area. When it did start up again the police would repeat the process. This was originally what constituted crime prevention.

Nowadays such procedure is no longer conceivable. Not only because the courts say these methods are a violation of an individual's rights (as they are) but because the use of these police methods, more than anything else, has led to the civil disorders and rioting of the sixties. A new day has dawned in old Dixie and throughout the country, often without police or public being fully cognizant of it.

Now the police must respond. Our procedure must be within the letter of the law. No more graphic illustration of this change in procedure can be seen than the vast difference in the way the police handled Oswald and, five years later,

113

Sirhan. It is not a question of different police departments. It reflects rather the tremendous change in police procedure throughout the country.

On an everyday basis how are the police operating? The process of investigation requires a more careful approach and a time-consuming attention to detail. It is necessary now and will be mandatory in the future that police detectives have law degrees. More personnel will be required to make arrests, to conduct painstaking investigations and prepare cases that meet all the requirements of the legal system.

The case goes to the courts for trial and the individual, if guilty, to the penal system for incarceration. Suppose after much lengthy and painstaking police work a burglar is arrested, tried and convicted, and sent to prison. And suppose that within two years' time he is out on parole. The odds are that in less than a year the police will have him again for committing a similar crime. For practically all major crimes are committed by repeaters—that is, by persons who have been imprisoned before for a similar crime. The system does not seem to deter criminals. Capital punishment does not reduce crime but neither does putting people in prison reduce crime. Seemingly prison does nothing but increase criminal tendencies. I am sure that every chief of police and head of the detective division in all major police departments in the country could sit down and work up a list where from five hundred to a thousand persons were rounded up and placed behind bars. Crime would drop to about zero—for a while.

It is demoralizing for the police to have to arrest the same people over and over again; futility and frustration enervate the entire police apparatus. We simply must find a new way of dealing with this situation, as the present system does not reduce crime but increases it.

I do not mean the police are opposed to rehabilitation and

parole of criminals. I am simply saying that thus far the present system that society supports with its tax dollars is wholly inadequate and we are going to have to spend a great deal more on converting criminals into law-abiding citizens.

At this point I can imagine the backlash reaction. Society does not reward people who obey the law, for they are expected to do just that. Then why should it reward violators of the law? The only answer I can give is another question: why should a country like the United States have financed the rehabilitation of Germany and Japan after World War II? But we did so, for at that time it was deemed to be in our best interest. Had we not done so the world would not have been a safe place in which to live. Our society cannot remain a healthy place in which to live if it continues to tolerate oppression and poverty in its midst. How many more eruptions within our cities must we suffer before we realize this?

7

Court Decisions

Nothing has altered police methods more in this country than recent Supreme Court decisions. The Mallory case, the Escobedo case, the Mapp case, and the Miranda case have been widely discussed in legal and police circles and by the American public generally.

Innumerable articles have been written on these cases and many speeches made, both pro and con. For generations to come the names of Mallory, Escobedo, Mapp, and Miranda will immediately bring to the minds of Americans some of the most significant reasons for social change in America in the sixties.

The decisions of the Supreme Court in these cases will have just as far-reaching an effect on our society as the civil rights decisions of the Court, if not more so. Nothing save the actual writing of the Constitution itself has had more influence on the relation of the police to American society. For

117

these decisions have changed the relationship between police and citizen in a fundamental way.

The Supreme Court's decision in these four important cases has eliminated completely a previously time-honored police practice in this country: *custodial interrogation.* The term means that if the police *thought* a person had committed a certain crime (that is, if they had a suspect) he was taken into custody and brought to the police station where he would be questioned extensively about the crime in which he was regarded as a prime suspect. At this point he was not actually charged with any crime. He was merely kept in custody until he "confessed." This had been the procedure for years. Barring an unimpeachable eyewitness to a crime, it was the method used in all crime solving from bicycle theft to first-degree murder.

In different localities and under different conditions this method of custodial interrogation varied widely. In small towns and hamlets, where practically no other police methods were known, the interrogation was generally followed by the suspect's making a statement of guilt followed by an announcement by the police that a "written confession" had been secured. As far as local police were concerned, this closed the case and sent the matter on to the courts. The theory here was that for every crime committed the police must, within a not too lengthy period of time, come up with the guilty party.

If it was a serious crime, such as murder committed against some prominent individual, the pressure on the police to come up with the murderer could be very great. It became a part of police legend that in important criminal cases especially the police came up with a suspect quickly, placed him under the bright lights, and by working day and night sweated out a confession. If the police did not follow this procedure and turn up a guilty party, then heads began to roll

118

around the old station house. The press would insist that the cops were incompetent; if they were not they would have found the culprit long ago.

The citizens of the community would become aroused and to save his own job the chief of police would relieve all those working on the case and give it to others with the dire instructions that they "sure as hell" better come up with a suspect. And if they did not, then the chief himself might soon be looking for another job.

Under the circumstances it is easy to see how the police in America began to rely strongly upon the method of custodial interrogation. It produced the desired results. The victim, his relatives, the press, the leaders of the community, all demanded immediate solutions. In such an atmosphere it was the only method open to harried police officials.

In the past in the South the most terrible crime that could be committed was that of rape or attempted rape of a white woman by a black man. In the smaller towns particularly the police would find themselves subject to intolerable pressures. The victim, relatives, press, and public demanded that the guilty party be brought to quick and speedy trial. If the police did not act quickly to apprehend the guilty party, citizens or vigilante groups would do so, or threaten to do so. The police *had* to come up with a suspect.

It has been my experience in this regard that white Southerners invariably have difficulty distinguishing one Negro from another. The problem has been the result of generations of segregation: the Negro was "there" but not "seen." Thus in most cases the victim of such a crime committed under obviously hysterical conditions could not positively identify the assailant. If she was sure that he was a black man, then she could not usually be sure of much else; and the victim was under the same pressure as everyone else to come up with the guilty man. When confronted by the "lineup" if she

119

"thought" so-and-so "looked" like the guilty one, then most police were often only too eager and willing to help her decide for sure that the person who she *thought* was the guilty party was indeed the person who *had* committed the crime. It has been my experience that quite often the assailant was incorrectly identified.

But if the police had a suspect that the victim was pretty certain was the guilty party, the police knew they had a good case. Mostly they were correct. Very swiftly the individual so identified was indicted, tried, and sentenced justly or unjustly with dispatch.

In these cases society demanded swift retribution, and if the police did not come up with the guilty party they always ran the risk of having the administration of justice taken out of their hands and assumed by the community—through kangaroo courts, hangings, and lynchings. The long record of these excesses in our history is too abundant to recount here.

The failure of the white Southerners to "see" Negroes as individuals has been one of the chief causes for the discrimination against Negroes in not only the South but the entire nation. Too often law enforcement officials assumed that to be black was to be marked by 50 percent or more of the guilt to begin with. Too often the attitude was that if the suspect was not guilty of a particular crime he was probably guilty of many other crimes for which he had never been held accountable or properly punished. He was black; most crimes of this type were committed by black people; ergo, one black man was as good as another to play the guilty part! In some instances it was considered that putting the particular individual out of circulation for a while would not be an infringement of justice and would contribute to law and order within the community. The police did not see themselves as contributing to injustice but to justice, for the Negro living in a high crime neighborhood was considered suspect by virtue

120

of being a member of a minority group.

This stigma extended not only to the individual but to his children and their children. Veterans of police work know families who have been criminals for two and three generations. It is not amazing, I think, for people who have relatives who are criminals to become criminals themselves. If a person's father owns a store it is not unlikely to see his son working there as a young man and taking the business over someday. This follows the usual middle-class way of life.

To people living in poverty who might happen to belong to some ethnic minority, it sometimes seems their best and only way to move up in the world is through crime. Some consider it the thing to do. Fortunately, many people born into high crime neighborhoods do not. Many outstanding police officers, in recent years, have come from this background. How they make this transition is for psychologists and sociologists to explain, as I am merely a witness that it does happen. What we in police work must do is to help make it happen more often.

The inability of whites to identify Negroes is but one example that recent Supreme Court decisions have had the effect of remedying. The case of mistaken identity is a part of all kinds of crimes that police departments must confront daily. No matter what type of crime is involved, if it is truly a situation in which the victim has no prior knowledge of who committed the crime against him it is extremely difficult to get an accurate identification.

A person with no knowledge that a crime is about to be committed against him is unlikely to be able to say afterwards who the guilty party is or make an accurate identification. The reason is obvious: the person is unaware and unsuspecting. He is going about his normal activity, other things are on his mind, and he does not foresee that he might be robbed, attacked, or otherwise involved in a crime. When it happens

121

it is a shock and he is unprepared to give an account of what happened or to recall with much clarity what his assailant looked like.

The same situation occurs in traffic accidents. Too few people think they are likely prospects, although they are far more likely to be involved in an accident than in a crime. As they drive along they may be thinking about business affairs, getting the children to school on time, or not being late for work. If they are involved in an accident they usually find it very difficult to be precise or coherent about exactly what happened.

The point of all this is that identification by a victim is too often too inaccurate a means of assistance in a modern police procedure. In all of these landmark cases, the Supreme Court has stated that the police simply cannot rely on this method as evidence to take a case to court for trial.

In getting back to the business of custodial interrogation, we might question whether or not it is really out the window and if so how the rights of the victim are to be maintained in the light of such Court rulings.

The first of these Supreme Court decisions, which many critics allege to be unprecedented, began with the arrest of Andrew R. Mallory for rape, in Washington, D.C., on April 7, 1954. (Interestingly, Mallory was arrested at about the same time as the Supreme Court was handing down its historic school desegregation ruling.) Mallory was detained in jail in Washington and charged with rape. After considerable questioning (custodial interrogation) Mallory admitted the charge and was later tried and convicted. Three years later, in 1957, the Supreme Court reversed the conviction and stated that "A suspect must be taken before a magistrate without delay. Any unnecessary delay will invalidate a confession obtained from the accused person prior to his appearance before a magistrate."

The Mallory case is a clear example of what has been previously discussed. It does not really reflect upon the guilt or innocence of Mallory but upon the methods employed by the police in the case. At the time the Court ruled in the Mallory case, police departments throughout the country were operating exactly as the Washington police did; that is, pick up a suspect and bring him in to the police station for grilling. The Supreme Court in its ruling was saying to all policemen everywhere that this type of procedure was at variance with the Constitution and had to cease.

A storm of protest naturally followed the Mallory decision. There were charges that such a decision would handicap the police and allow rapists and murderers to roam the streets free. To keep this from happening it became incumbent on police to find new and different procedures to bring these people to justice. The court was not saying, as some critics implied, that such criminals could escape due process of law. It was saying the exact opposite: every American, regardless of whether he was a rapist, murderer, or other criminal, was entitled to his rights under the Constitution. A person guilty of a crime could not be brought to justice through illegal means, no matter how terrible the crime committed.

What did this imply about police procedures in the future? It meant that police would have to investigate more fully, talk with more witnesses to the crime or people with some knowledge of the circumstances surrounding the crime. It required that a person's guilt be established through careful police methods. This further meant that in the future there would of necessity be need for more and better trained police investigators. It also implied that society would have to be aware of the new procedure (some called it undue hardships) that the police were now compelled to follow in cases of this nature.

It has already been pointed out that a crime such as rape

123

usually generates passionate demands by the press and the general public for a speedy solution. Society now has to realize as the police have to acknowledge that in a complex case where no unimpeachable eyewitness is available or a confession by the guilty offered, the establishing of guilt or innocence may not be a matter of days or weeks but of months or years. This may often result in a very slow implementation of justice, yet as is implied in the Court's decision no justice is infinitely better than injustice.

Too often the public has been aroused to castigate the Court for the ruling. The public has demanded to know how the Court's decision affected the victim of rape. What are the victim's rights? Surely the rights of the victim should take precedence over those of the criminal!

The original case against Mallory involved an attempt by society, through its agent—the police—to see that society's obligation to guarantee the rights of the victim were carried out. The entire police apparatus in the Mallory case was an effort to do something about the violation of the victim's rights.

But in their zeal to safeguard the victim's rights the police unduly abused the rights of the allegedly guilty party. The courts did not say that the police could not be aggressive in safeguarding a victim's rights; they could not be aggressive in abusing the rights of the allegedly guilty party.

The next case ruled on by the Supreme Court, the Escobedo case, is probably better known to the general public than the Mallory case. Daniel Escobedo was arrested in Chicago, Illinois, on January 19, 1960, and charged with murder. He asked for an attorney and his attorney asked to see him. Both requests were denied. Later he confessed and was tried and convicted. In 1964 the Supreme Court reversed the conviction and stated: "A person has a right to an attorney and the right to remain silent."

"I must warn you . . . that anything you may say will be used against you in court. . . ." Many times the American public has heard this or a similar phrase on radio or television. In movies involving crime a Hollywood idol was always advising the person in the police station that he had better be careful about what he said for it could be used against him.

Every American should always have been aware that the right to remain silent was a basic right, guaranteed by the Constitution and confirmed by the entertainment industry in this country. But too many of us in police work in practice often disregarded this basic right. If we had a prime suspect, the best way for harassed, understaffed police departments to gain a confession was to hold the suspect until he confessed.

As a result of the Escobedo case, the police must now devote a great deal of time and effort into making the case against the accused. There is no more custodial interrogation without the accused being aware of his rights and of his right to counsel to advise him. To accuse a person legally the police now may not rely upon the cooperation of the accused, for that is a violation of his rights.

On the face of it, this decision appears a more complete departure from past procedures than the Mallory case, or those which followed. For adequately staffed and trained police personnel it did not make much difference. Long before the Escobedo case the courts had been throwing out cases which relied solely on a "station house" confession that was later recanted in court, as the best case a lawyer could make for his client under these conditions was that the accused had not been properly advised of his rights.

In most cases the police knew it was not best to rely on this police method. But the police are often overworked and the backlog of cases awaiting their attention is often as great as those awaiting court action. The granting of a confession by

125

the accused was the fastest way for the police to get the case out of the department and into the courts. But, as said before, the courts often refused to allow such procedures to stand up.

Public outcry following the Escobedo decision was greater than that following any other such decisions. Critics said the Escobedo decision made it too easy for criminals to elude justice; it was not a police function to determine guilt or innocence; if the police made a mistake, the person had recourse to the courts; let the courts decide; too many guilty ones would go free if it was made more difficult for the police to arrest people and get them into court.

Anyone who has been in police work very long will quickly tell you that hardened criminals and professional crooks know all about their rights and knew about them before the Escobedo case. They didn't tell the police anything before the Escobedo case and haven't since the Escobedo case except to say they wanted to see their lawyer. Their legal counsel was also well aware of the law, what rights the accused had, and what rights the police possessed. The Escobedo case has not caused people who formerly "blabbed" to suddenly clam up. The type of person who confessed before the Escobedo case still does so. Such a person's desire to tell the police, or anyone who will listen, that he has committed a crime comes from some inner compulsion with little assistance from the police.

An example of the use of the lineup relates to previous discussion concerning the identity of criminals and how difficult it is for victims to identify assailants who are strangers to them. A victim will be brought in to view the lineup. He will see several people and be asked if he can identify any one of them as his assailant. Sometimes he can do so, but often the victim will identify the desk sergeant as the person who committed the crime.

126

On the other hand, it happens, more often than you might think, that the assailant identifies himself to the victim and to the police! We in police work see it happen quite often. Why the assailant does this is not actually known. Maybe the desire to be better known, the compulsion to confess guilt, the confrontation with his victim, the pressure of suspense, or other unknown factors contribute to this personal identification.

Incidentally, most modern police lineups now use various lighting techniques to simulate actual conditions under which the crime was committed. If a person was robbed on a poorly lighted street or in darkness, his assailant is not going to look the same under glaring lights.

In the light of the Escobedo case, the police still use the lineup without denial of legal counsel. There is nothing in this decision which denies the judge the right to set bond at whatever amount he thinks justified. In the Mallory case, while ruling out custodial interrogation, the Court did not rule out the right of police to take people into custody and utilize the lineup later, so long as the individual was apprised of his rights.

Another case of much current interest was the Mapp case. Mrs. Dollree Mapp was arrested in Cleveland, Ohio, on May 23, 1957, after police officers forced their way into her home without a warrant and found obscene material. The police denied her attorney entry during the search, nor would they permit Mrs. Mapp to see him. She was later tried and convicted.

In 1961 the U. S. Supreme Court reversed the conviction and stated that evidence cannot be used in any court if collected during a search and seizure that is unreasonable or illegal. The Mapp case is significant because it concerns illegal activity carried out in the home of the suspect. In the

Mapp case it applied to the possession of allegedly obscene material, but the case has far-reaching repercussions in cases involving gambling activities.

Freedom from unreasonable search and seizure in one's home is based on ancient English common-law rights. It had its origin in the attempt of the people to protect themselves from intrusion and the seizure of property by unrestrained kings and rulers.

A man's home is his castle and yet no person can use his home as a base for illegal activity. Gambling is a serious virus that has always attacked the body politic. People who want to gamble find various ways to do so. When a person is engaged in illegal gambling activity in his house, it is no longer his home or his castle but a place of business, in fact an illegal business. The police have an obligation to move in and put a stop to the activity to protect law-abiding citizens of the community.

Before they move in, however, they must spend long hours of surveillance of those who enter and leave, checking identifications and gathering other information for building up their case. Then they must have proper search and seizure warrants from the courts before they move in. How much less bothersome it would be for the police, when they get a tip, to rush out and raid a house where the suspected illegal gambling activity was being conducted. It would save a lot of work and effort and everybody could go home at five o'clock like other people who have regular eight-to-five jobs. In modern police work it doesn't work out this way.

Much illegal gambling activity is now conducted by electronic means. Since we live in an age of technology, the criminal element in our society also makes use of the sophisticated machines that a technological society provides. The most prevailing use is that of electronic communication: the telephone. In this age a multimillion-dollar gambling enterprise can be carried out in a house or office with a mere desk and telephone. In such an operation there are no suspicious characters going in and out indicating to anyone who might see them that there is illegal activity inside. Most police information in such cases comes from conscientious citizens who have seen something that seems phony or looks suspicious. Modern communication methods make it harder for anyone, either the ordinary citizens or the police, to detect improper or illegal activities from outside appearance.

I am of the opinion that police, acting under orders of the court, must have the right to tune in on the conducting of illegal activities over the telephone, while at the same time I am aware of the potential abuse of the rights and privacy of the individual through the use of wiretapping. With all the drawbacks involved, I think the police should have use of this tool.

First, the mere knowledge by the gamblers that the police have this power to carry out wiretapping puts them at a disadvantage. With this awareness, the criminal will be less inclined to conduct illegal activity over the telephone. This forces him more out into the open, subjecting him to public and police view.

Second, wiretapping can be responsibly used to combat interlocking elements of crime from one city or section of the country to another. When this is used as a police tool, criminals cannot as easily join forces to swindle and abuse the rights of other citizens. The ability of the local hoodlum to connect his activities to a chainlike criminal operation is lessened. Can you imagine chain stores or branch banks being able to operate without electronic communication? The same is true of large-scale illegal activity. Cut into their means of communication and you have gone a long way toward reducing this type of criminal activity.

Wiretapping, however, is loaded with the possibility of

129

abuse; more so than any other police procedure. The secret of the success of any police weapon or tool is in the certainty that it does not lead to abuse.

I recall a case some years back when a very attractive young woman came into my office to lodge a complaint of rape against a young police officer. When I inquired about the details she told me that she and her boy friend had been parked out on a lonely road late at night. A patrol car came cruising by and beamed a light on them. The policeman got out of his car and forced the girl to get into the police car. He told the boy to leave and not to come back or to say anything to anyone; if he did so he (the policeman) would "get him."

When I arranged for the three people to meet around a table in my office, the girl told her story again and repeated it in the same manner as previously. I turned to the boy and demanded to know why he had not immediately called the police. He replied that the police were there already! From his point of view there was nothing else he could do. The boy was only eighteen and had been in trouble with the police when he was much younger for stealing change out of a self-service newspaper-vending machine. He said he felt if the police "got it in" for him again they would really make it hard for him the next time. He was frightened and so intimidated by police power that he did as the policeman told him and had done and said nothing to anyone.

As it developed later, the girl had formerly been a friend of the policeman's. He denied having sexual relations with her on this occasion. After more lengthy discussion the girl admitted what the policeman said was true. They had gone together, broken up, and had had a heated argument that night on the lonely road. She was now trying to get back at him by using the charge of rape. Regardless of the details of the case, she pointed out that the policeman had had no right to force her companion away that night. This was intimidation, as I readily agreed. The policeman resigned promptly.

The charge of intimidation is often lodged against a police officer who is investigating a case which is going against the accused. With the exception of this one incident, in my experience the charge has always proved to be utterly groundless.

In this case a person's rights (the boy's more than the girl's) were abused by the unwarranted and illegal use of police power. A similar danger is inherent in wiretapping. Listening in electronically on private conversations could lead to the same kind of abuse of an individual's rights. The real danger in wiretapping, however, is not that the police will abuse the power but that it is used and being greatly abused by private groups.

It is not too difficult to tap a telephone. People other than the telephone company can tune in on your telephone conversations. Suppose a husband and wife are involved in a divorce action and one hires a lawyer or investigator to get evidence on the other. If need be, and for the right price, they can locate someone capable of tapping the telephone line. The potentiality for blackmail here is obvious and a far greater danger to a person's rights than any tapping activity carried out by the police.

Acting under orders of the courts, I am convinced, the police must have the right to carry out wiretapping activities. It is the most effective way to combat crime in America and the American people should have confidence that the police will carry out these activities with the utmost regard for the rights of the individual. The requirement that a court order be secured before each wiretapping activity of the police protects the civil rights and rights to privacy of the individual.

The subject matter in the Mapp case did not concern illegal gambling activity but the possession of alleged obscene material. This involves a topic for consideration of consider-

131

able complexity and public debate: pornography. In the case of so-called pornography, the police have another nearly impossible situation on their hands. The police must look to the community and the courts for guidance and, in this instance, the opinions are often divided. In light of these conflicting opinions about what is and is not obscene, how are the police supposed to react?

The situation is not unlike the civil rights conflict. When segregation was the law of the land any Negro drinking out of a "white only" water fountain could be arrested for violating the law. There was a time, too, when, if a distributor was found to be selling books describing explicit sex or containing pictures of naked people, his establishment could be raided and closed. Now this procedure is no longer possible.

We, the Atlanta Police Department, try to rely on persuasion. That is to say, when we receive a complaint we talk with the owners of the various book outlets and try to persuade them to withdraw reading material that is offensive to the segments of the public that have brought such complaints to the police. More often than not the distributor (also caught in the confusion of what is and is not obscene) will cooperate. Yet the furor has not subsided, although I suspect the matter is more of a problem in the heart of the so-called Bible Belt than in other areas of the country.

Several years ago seldom a day passed when some irate citizen did not call me to complain about a certain book which had been brought to his attention and which was, in his opinion, highly pornographic and immoral. The parting shot invariably was "Would you want your son or daughter reading such filth?" This never failed to remind me of that other now defunct sally, "Would you want your daughter to marry one?"

The issue remains a highly emotional one, not only in the matter of books but also movies. The Atlanta city government

132

has adopted an ordinance making it illegal to sell obscene literature to minors. This follows the same legal path as the law forbidding the sale of alcoholic beverages to minors. I think it is a good law. Book distributors who now sell what is described (and the police make no attempt to do this, for it is the function of the judiciary) as pornographic literature must keep these books out of view of minors or sealed so that they are not available to minors. This procedure has two good features, as I see it. It makes no attempt to restrict or prohibit what an adult may or may not read while at the same time it keeps books "without any redeeming social value" out of the hands of minors. In the main the distributors have been pleased with the new law.

Of course, books of this nature would not be available if there were not people wanting to buy them. The people who sell these books do so for one reason—to make money. If there was no profit in the business they would not be in business. From reports I receive, their business is booming.

If I seem to treat this matter of "dirty books" too lightly, it is probably because I believe that so-called dirty books have only (if any) a negligible relation to criminal activity and to breaking the law.

The theory in some quarters is that people who read such books are likely to go out and do whatever is described in the books. If this is the case then people who are exposed to violence on television are far more likely to go out and be violent, television being a much more personal medium and form of communication. As far as the influence of dirty books and violence on television toward people breaking the law and committing violent acts is concerned, I would pretty much discount this. Criminal acts and crimes of violence, to my way of thinking, are far more individually inspired and arise from sources within each individual regardless of his taste in books and television viewing.

133

About the only direct way that I can see that violence between individuals has resulted from watching television would be if during an argument over what program to watch one of the persons concerned, in a moment of anger, picked up the set and heaved it at his antagonist. *This* has happened. In most cases, though, the antagonized person would be more likely to reach for a gun, and current statistics indicate a firearm would likely be near at hand.

From the standpoint of police enforcement of the law the habit a large segment of the American people displays of reading so-called dirty books, watching violent shows on television, and buying guns in record-breaking quantity says something about their character. This tendency concerns the police significantly. If all those whose "prurient interests" are satisfied by reading dirty books, whose inclination to beat someone is whetted by an actor getting his face bashed in on television, or if all the people who possessed guns actually attempted to settle their disagreements by using them, the present overwhelming police problem would be pale in comparison!

The last of the Supreme Court decisions which have radically changed police practice and procedure in America is the Miranda case. Whenever I have made a speech or been questioned by the press in the past several years the question of the Miranda case has always come up.

Ernesto Miranda was arrested in Phoenix, Arizona, on March 3, 1963. He was detained in the Phoenix jail and charged with kidnaping and rape. After considerable questioning, he admitted the charge. He was tried and convicted. In 1966 the U.S. Supreme Court reversed the conviction on the grounds that he was not advised of his right to counsel and the right to remain silent.

Again I cannot agree with those who think the Miranda case has handicapped police in any manner. Like the others,

134

however, this case has made police work more complex because once more it slams the door on custodial interrogation. This decision states that the police *must* advise the accused of his right to remain silent and of his right to adequate legal counsel, and further declares he must be provided with a lawyer if without one.

As has been pointed out, hardened criminals are so well aware of the law that often their lawyer is at the police station by the time the accused is in custody. All the Court has said in this case is that knowledgeable people and others wealthy enough to have legal representation are not the only ones, in a democratic society, who are entitled to legal representation. Everyone is entitled to legal aid and if the police want a case to stand up in court they had better be sure that the accused knows what his legal rights are and that he is represented by counsel.

Many people feel that the recent Court decisions are wrong and should be changed, believing they restrict the police in fighting crime and the courts in bringing criminals to justice. At this period in our history I believe that to revert to the old ways would be tragic.

The Court decisions of the past ten years have shaken police procedure in the area where it needs shaking. It has, understandably, shaken the police officer's confidence in himself to be told by the highest legal authority that police practice is shopworn and undemocratic. It is little wonder that he has sometimes reacted with indignation and outrage.

The criticism of police practice implied in the Supreme Court decisions is also a rebuke and criticism of the lower courts. If the police and the courts had been more careful of their own duties over the years, then perhaps the decision of the Supreme Court would not have been necessary. I am convinced that neither the police nor the lower courts intended to abuse the law. But over the years tradition and lack of impetus for change brought about this situation. In order to rectify the situation and comply fully with the Supreme Court decisions much needs to be done.

Life in the latter part of this century requires that police use methods more in keeping with the times. Methods employed in the past will no longer suffice. These new methods require new policemen—policemen who are better educated, better trained, and better oriented to the problems of life in this part of the century. This, in turn, requires that society be more *concerned* and more ready with the *cash* to see that police are made capable of utilizing the newer methods.

The police and the courts are parts of the same organism. I have no criticism of the Supreme Court and none of the lower courts. In most instances I think the lower courts have tried diligently to conform to the new guidelines necessitated by the Supreme Court decisions. If the Supreme Court decisions are to be adequately carried out, however, the attention and cooperation the police are seeking must also be accorded the courts. In the lower courts we need judges of the highest caliber and must provide salaries adequate to attract the best persons in the legal profession.

In the Atlanta Police Department we have been successful in conforming to the guidelines outlined by the Supreme Court as a result of the assistance we have received from the judges in the lower courts here. For example, many judges in this area have taken it upon themselves to be available to the police literally twenty-four hours a day. In many cases this is crucial.

Since the Escobedo decision states that an accused person must be brought before a magistrate without undue delay, suppose it is two o'clock in the morning and the police have a suspect in custody with his lawyer there demanding that

136

the police release his client unless they have specific charges to bring against him. In this instance a magistrate is required.

Suppose the police wish to make a raid in the middle of the night and to delay could mean that the suspects might not be engaged in their illegal activity by morning? Since the Mapp case says that "evidence cannot be used in any court if collected in a search that is unreasonable or illegal," the police must go to the judge, even if the hour is not convenient, to secure a warrant. Obviously this places an enormous burden on the judges. Atlanta police have been greatly helped by such men who place the maintenance of good law enforcement in the community above their own personal convenience.

But this is only a piecemeal solution. Adequate means must be provided by society to ensure court participation in these matters day and night. We have 24-hour-a-day policemen. We must have 24-hour-a-day judges.

I would be less than candid if I did not say that the Supreme Court's decisions have made the policeman's and the lower courts' jobs more strenuous. It would be much easier to return to the old ways but progress cannot be achieved without effort. In fact, the Supreme Court decisions do require more effort on the part of all of us in the law-enforcement field. As a consequence, society needs to be aware of this and be willing to give moral and financial support to ensure continuing effort.

In plain language this means that the federal government must provide money to aid us in conforming to these Court decisions. There is not now sufficient financial support on the state or local level to do the job. The federal government must become involved and accept its responsibility in this. There are approximately 420,000 police officers in the United States and the money required to maintain the police depart-

137

ments is approximately $2.5 billion annually. The federal government now contributes nothing to the support of these budgets.

On the other hand, there are approximately 400,000 National Guardsmen in this country with a budget of about half the budget for police departments and the federal government pays all the cost for supporting the National Guard. This is, of course, 1910 procedure and financing. It is unrealistic to expect to meet the problems of modern urban life in this way. Perhaps once it was necessary for the federal government to maintain the National Guard in order to give protection to those who lived on the frontier but it is not sufficient reason for people who live in today's society.

Crime is a national and not a local problem and should be so treated. For example, one of the major crimes is bank robbery. This is a federal offense but it certainly requires countless man-hours on the part of local police. Detectives in the Atlanta Police Department assigned to investigate bank robberies are doing the same job and are required to have the same background as the FBI man in the Atlanta office who works on bank robberies. Both men are doing an outstanding job, yet the federal man makes much more money than the Atlanta detective. All of the FBI man's salary is paid by the federal government. Shouldn't part of the detective's salary be paid by the federal government also? Our practices in this regard need to be made more realistic. The time for doing so is late. If the federal government continues to remain uninvolved, it does so at our peril.

8

The Increase of Crime

We in the Atlanta Police Department have had to make few changes to bring the procedures of the department into line with the Supreme Court decisions. Most of the changes have merely been an intensification of our efforts in the direction we were already moving. Orders and operations that were once carried out orally now must be written out and substantiated. This requires more time and more people. We also have instituted a departmental policy that all crime reports must follow a rigidly prescribed written form.

We spend twice as much time training people to follow the Court guidelines and twice as much time gathering information and securing warrants as before. All cases must be carefully prepared and made airtight.

Does this mean that our arrest record has suffered as a result? Not at all. Our arrest and "clear-up" record is better than it has ever been. The Supreme Court decisions have had the effect of *making better policemen out of all of us*. We are now doing things correctly whereas in the past we might have been haphazard in collecting information and gathering evidence for a case.

It is true that the entire procedure adds to a policeman's actual working time. Imagine that a suspect has been brought into the lineup. His lawyer has been notified but is not present. The entire procedure must be held up while the police take time to locate the lawyer. Often we have to go out and bring the lawyer to the police station. Old-timers would have died laughing had anyone suggested that such a thing was actually a police function. But in police work we find out every day that we have functions we never dreamed we had. We do our best to meet them.

In following the Supreme Court guidelines the police method most expanded has been the use of scientific analysis in solving crimes. We now have to go over the crime scene much more carefully than we ever did before and we make use of more and better techniques of examination.

Take the matter of fingerprints as an example. For a long time the lifting of latent fingerprints at the crime scene was of little value because of the man-hours required in attempting to match such prints by hand. But everybody knew about fingerprints and if a person had a burglary at his home or office he certainly expected the police to get fingerprints. The police would do so with the full knowledge that the prints were of little value. The whole business was more of a public relations tool than a helpful police investigative procedure.

Recent advances in technology have changed this. Our Identification Bureau installed Recordak Micracode Microfilm equipment in May, 1968. The bureau began converting the "Single-hand Fingerprint Files" to the new equipment. By December of that year, 14,000 sets of fingerprints were converted to the new system. The system searches latent fingerprints found at a crime scene against fingerprints of known offenders of whom we have records for similar crimes. This mechanized system has many advantages over the manual system previously used. It can use the additional codes which we have developed, thereby cutting searching time. Use of the new codes is not practical under the manual system, but it is possible to use additional descriptive data. The system has the ability to use all latents at one time rather than searching only for one. Fingerprints are projected on the screen and can be compared at this point. Five hundred fifty persons can be processed into each 100 feet of film. At the time the film is developed positive and negative copies are made. The positive copy is placed into a film magazine which is acceptable to the retrieving device. The retriever has code keyboards which allow the search to be keyed into the machine. It takes only ten seconds for the retriever to scan 550 fingerprint cards. When the machine locates a card that has codes matching requested information, it automatically stops and projects the fingerprint card on the viewing screen. We are now in the process of extending the service to include a modus operandi file on offenders in certain crime categories.

This is a magnificent device modern science has given us in fighting crime. Contrary to what most people imagine about the average criminal and his knowledge of police procedure, criminals do leave fingerprints behind more often than not.

Or, as another example of improved technique, take the matter of identification. It used to be routine to have a victim come in and look through books of "mug shots" of previous offenders in an attempt to identify his assailant. Now we use color slides flashed on a screen. These slides are of course much more lifelike than the mug shots and help a victim identify his assailant.

141

We also use color photography at all crime scenes today. Later studies of these color slides by police and victims may turn up details missed in the rush and confusion of the time immediately following a crime. This is especially true if violence was involved.

At the crime scene itself, because our officers have been more scientifically trained, interviews with the people involved have been improved and this generally turns up a witness otherwise unknown to the victim.

But along with advances in police technique has come an increase in crime. Every month local police departments send crime statistics to the FBI. Quarterly the FBI in Washington releases figures on crime in the various localities. The FBI is of course the proper organization to do this; however, it should be pointed out that the FBI does not *gather* this information, but merely compiles and releases to the public information which has been passed on from local police departments throughout the nation. It must be remembered, too, that this information is only as accurate and reliable as the police departments which submit it. In the past, it was not unheard of for some departments to be sloppy in their record keeping, and even guilty of watering down crime statistics in an attempt to boost their local images as avid crime fighters.

Although crime is on the increase, there is very little new about the increase in crime. They are the same types of crime which have been committed for decades—just more of them.

A crime which has skyrocketed in numbers in recent years is that of homicide. The homicide rate is rising faster than the rate of growth of the over-all population. What can the police do about this situation?

Almost 70 percent of all homicides occur in the home, where the assailant is known to the victim. Homicides happen most frequently as a result of arguments about money,

142

fights between men and women, and often when lots of liquor is being consumed. Homicides occur in the home for all kinds of domestic reasons. I have known of cases in which one person shot another because he didn't like the way the other closed the door. The victim is nearly always a relative, certainly an acquaintance, of the assailant.

This type of crime can best be reduced by reducing the number of lethal weapons, that is, guns, available to people. Of the 183 homicides committed in the city of Atlanta in 1968 the weapons used were:

Pistols	109
Shotguns	13
Rifles	6
Knives	35
Other	20

Therefore, of the 183 homicides committed in Atlanta that year 128 were committed with some type of firearm. If this is not sufficient argument for some kind of weapons control among the civilian population, I do not know what is.

Most homicides are unplanned. They occur on the spur of the moment and are generally crimes of passion and/or anger. Other than urging a reduction in the number of guns available to people there is little the police can do to prevent these crimes. It is more a question that addresses itself to psychologists and sociologists and the general public than to the police. Only this kind of interest from all of society will reduce the number of homicides very much.

Our rate of solving homicides remains steady. While the homicide rate goes up, the police find out who is responsible at an even greater rate. Unfortunately this does not seem to make the spiraling rate itself go down. To a police officer who has long believed that the certainty of punishment is the best deterrent to crime this causes some wonder. But I do not think future generations are going to be restrained from

143

crimes such as homicide because of the certainty of punishment. It is going to take some other kind of deterrent or treatment. The police stand ready to join forces with all segments of society in the attempt to bring about the reduction of homicide. Some new ideas are badly needed on the subject.

Another problem in preventing crime goes back to that old bugaboo we talked about in relation to wiretapping: *technology*. Because of the rapid availability and increase in the means of transportation in our society, crime no longer follows city, state, or regional lines. As modern technology has so greatly improved the speed and availability of transportation, so it has at the same time contributed to the increase in crime. A criminal can rob a bank in California and be in Oklahoma in a matter of hours. This means that the police must not be restrained by state, county, or regional boundaries. The police must go where the criminals go.

Does this mean we must have a national police force? This bears much thought but I can say this: if we are serious about doing anything about crime in the United States we *must* have national standards of enforcement and the means of communication among all government enforcement agencies, local, state, and federal.

In the sixties an enormous police problem was car theft. It is still a problem, certainly, but now in the seventies it seems to be leveling off in some areas. Why? I believe our success in Atlanta in lessening this type of criminal activity is due to the setting up of a regional clearinghouse for police problems. The Metropolitan Police, or Metropol, is an organization to which all city and county police departments within the greater Atlanta area belong. This includes some fifty police and sheriff departments in this area. Metropol is the only known organization of its type in the country. The needed staff support and funds are furnished by the Metropolitan Atlanta Council of Local Governments. The departments

144

who participate do not pay dues; everything is done on a voluntary basis.

There is teletype communication between all member departments of Metropol, and if an automobile is stolen in one section of the area all the police departments know about it simultaneously and can immediately be on the lookout for this automobile. This closed-circuit teletype system started out with twelve stations but has now been expanded to statewide coverage, giving each station direct contact with the National Crime Information Center (NCIC) located in Washington, D.C. If a car is stolen in California, the report on this stolen vehicle is sent to the NCIC in Washington. If a car with a California tag turns up in Georgia, the police can contact NCIC and know in a matter of minutes if the car is stolen or not. In the past getting such information meant a delay of days or weeks, and speed in the matter of apprehending criminals is of the utmost importance. Criminals take quick advantage of any delay on the part of police officials.

Another factor that has helped in reducing car theft is the cooperation of the car manufacturers themselves. Car identification numbers are now placed in a position where they can be seen easily by the police checking an auto. This does not require a warrant should the car be locked. Going for a warrant takes time and during the delay the criminal might easily leave the area. The placing of steering locks on all new cars and the elimination of vent windows is another way in which car manufacturers are attempting to make car theft more difficult. Also buzzer locks and serial numbers on component parts of the automobile are a big help. There is much criminal activity involved in stripping parts from automobiles. The police can now check out the salvage of these parts and be on the lookout for the types of parts stolen from the cars. All of these measures have made things more difficult for the car thief.

145

Automobile owner awareness also has aided in the reduction of car theft. The public seems to be aware that certain automobiles are much more likely to be stolen, depending on the year and make of the car, and take the necessary precautions.

Metropol is involved in many activities besides car theft. There are intelligence meetings every week of the member departments of Metropol. Representatives from all departments get together once a week and literally swap information. If one department is working on a car theft or burglary ring, all the police officers go over the details very carefully to see if any similar crimes in their own areas are in any way related to the criminal activity taking place in someone else's jurisdiction. This is the only way to do anything about crime in modern America.

Metropol has organized an effective training program for the various departments on a cooperative basis. The training program started in June, 1965. Some of the schools and seminars held are as follows:

SCHOOLS CONDUCTED		OFFICERS ATTENDING
4	100–Hour Recruit	230
1	40–Hour Recruit	39
1	200–Hour Recruit	29
12	70–Hour Recruit	292
1	35–Hour Management	124
3	105–Hour School, Conducted by Northwestern Traffic Institute	124
30	Seminars—National Crime Information Center	1,200

Many other officers attended various monthly seminars which covered all phases of police training efforts. The department provides specialists to lecture at many of the training sessions of Metropol.

The police have had to contend with an increasing number of bank robberies in recent years. Part of the reason for this rise has been the expansion of the banking business into the suburbs. At first the banks were concerned with making things convenient for their customers and little thought was given to the business of protecting the new operations, but making things convenient for the customers also made things easy for robbers. A small branch bank in the outer areas, often manned by only two or three people, becomes a prime setup for robbers. When these robberies began to occur with more and more frequency banks began to take strong measures to prevent them. The employment of full-time guards, the use of hidden cameras, and the awareness of bank employees have gone a long way toward reducing this type of crime.

Burglary of residences and businesses remains the most consistent kind of criminal activity. With our booming economy and continued good times for most and poverty for some, the availability of things for people to steal has grown enormously in recent years. Houses have so much in them these days! The temptation for people to get things through illegal means remains enormous. I can recall that in the early days of my police career the most likely item to be stolen in a house burglary was money. This was in a period when people could remember when banks had failed and did not trust the banks to keep their money. They felt their money was often safer at home. This made money the big item taken in burglaries during the thirties. It was there, literally hidden under the mattress, and the crooks went after it.

Nowadays because of the burgeoning crime in home burglaries people no longer keep cash in their homes, for they have become convinced that it isn't safe. Money is more likely to be stolen if kept at home rather than lost in a bank

147

failure. Frankly, I think anyone is unwise to keep small valuable items in the home: items such as jewelry of any value, coin collections, or objects of art of authentic value. It just isn't safe, and I think we should view these items just as we do money.

There are many other items kept at home for the thieves to go after. The "hot" items today are firearms of all kinds, radios and television sets, cameras, liquor, and expensive clothes. In short, merchandise and weapons. Many homes have as much merchandise in them as some stores contained in the thirties. Would-be criminals are sorely tempted by such riches.

The psychology in regard to burglary is important here. Whatever is "big" and in demand in the open market will be big items people want to steal. In other words, crime follows the market. When color television sets first appeared on the scene they quickly became number one on the burglary list. There was a huge demand for such sets. A person could steal them and sell them at a good price to others.

What all thieves ultimately want is money, and inasmuch as practically all money today is in banks, thieves steal things that can be most quickly turned into cash. If an item, such as a color TV set, is new on the market and in great demand, it can be converted into money very quickly.

When wigs first hit the market and began to be desired by a large segment of the consumer public, wig theft became a major police problem! How do you trace and identify a wig? No serial number, no indication of where the item was purchased, in fact little or no identification is possible. But in time wigs ceased to be a big item. The market was filled with them, people grew tired of the novelty; wig theft fell to almost zero.

I wonder how many can remember when hubcaps were the thing? In the fifties when the automobile dealers came

148

out with all those fancy "spinners" and "flyers" detective departments throughout the nation were worked to death trying to run down hubcap thieves and retrieve stolen spinners. The situation became so bad that an outraged public reacted by refusing to purchase hubcaps. It became the fad to buy a new car minus hubcaps. When the auto manufacturers realized what was happening they began changing designs and making hubcaps less of a desired theft item. Again, the problem of hubcap theft was greatly reduced and is no longer a police problem of much significance.

By the time this book is published the "hot" item will more than likely be something else, but as of this writing the most desired item and the one being stolen most frequently is the stereo tape recorder from an automobile. Where once the embattled and theft-weary citizen parked his car and worried it might be stolen or at least his hubcaps might be taken, he now is concerned, or should be, about the stereo tape recorder in his new automobile. The chances are the thief will ignore the car, certainly the hubcaps, but will yank out the tape recorder in a flash. Everybody wants a stereo recorder in his car. It is the current "thing." The "now" generation wants them. They can thus be disposed of quickly at a good price. It is a fast moneymaker for the criminal, as sure as a tip on a hot stock.

Just as we all do, the criminal in our society watches television, reads the newspapers, and sees all the new items appearing on the market. He desires these items either for his personal use or to convert into cash. Whereas the law-abiding citizen thinks about saving to acquire this new item and paying for it in installments or doing without something else in order to have it, the criminal will proceed to acquire the item by illegal means. The motivation is much the same. As a consumer, he wants a particular item and goes after it in a criminal way.

Now, when you see a new item on the market, desire it and begin thinking of ways of buying it, remember that the crook is thinking the same thoughts except he thinks in terms of illegal ways and means. When a new item appears and you as a faithful American consumer buy it, guard it carefully—for crooks are scheming night and day to get their hands on it. Whether it be yours or the property of some other citizen, the crooks are concerned only with getting what they want by stealing.

What does all this imply? It means that in the future we should have more stringent laws and more accurate control of goods produced in our society. Items must be labeled so that they can be readily identified. We must by national laws and regulations make it as difficult as possible for the criminal element in our society to steal from the rest of us. Studying and being aware that crime follows the market is as good a first step as I know of. Market and research analysis could check with police departments just as easily as they could with chain stores to know how a new item on the market is going over with the consumer. If sales are good at the stores, the theft of the item is going to be very "big" with local police departments.

The growth and prosperity of business throughout the country makes the theft of office equipment and business machines as good a business as business itself. Theft in businesses, particularly small concerns which do not have full-time security guards, is on the increase. The businesses are crammed with all types of modern electronic machines that our society produces to make the carrying on of business more efficient. Business equipment, such as typewriters and cash registers, is very high on the theft list. Such items can mean quick money for the criminal.

This means that all businesses should take every precaution to safeguard their goods and property. They must install the latest electronic burglar alarm equipment, and if at all possible keep close security on their buildings day and night. There can never be enough police to protect all the private merchandise and property in our growing economy. The individual businessman has had to assume more and more of this responsibility. He must be careful and more security conscious. Maybe such measures seem to indicate our society is becoming more controlled, more fearful of theft and burglary. This is probably true. But it is also true that if people themselves will take all the precautions possible they will have gone a long way toward protecting themselves from theft.

As in the case of automobile thefts, there is a clearinghouse maintained by the FBI concerned with burglary. The National Crime Information Center keeps a record of stolen items and places them on computer tape so that once something is recovered, even if in another state, the local police department can contact NCIC and know in a matter of minutes if the goods were stolen and where they were stolen. This is true too of all firearms.

What makes a person want to steal? Why is it that the overwhelming majority of people in society are willing to save and do without in order to acquire a particular thing, whereas others in society prefer to steal? If the police knew the answer to this, crime in America would not be the problem it is.

Perhaps we can determine why there is more of this type of illegal activity every year, even if we cannot determine the basic causes of thievery itself—which lawmen and philosophers have been trying to discover for centuries.

It is a complex matter but I think the desire to get something for nothing is a basic motivation to the criminal. Most of us wish to get something for as little cost to ourselves as possible. We do not want to pay an outrageous price. We shop around. We check prices. We go to the discount house. In this case the motivation of the ordinary, law-abiding citizen and that of the criminal seem to be different only in degree. The honest citizen wishes to get the best "deal" possible when buying a stereo tape recorder. The criminal wishes to get one for nothing. Follow this argument to its logical conclusion and you come up with the thought that solution of crime in our society rests upon abolishing society. Not a very likely possibility.

What I am saying is that the basic cause or motivation for crime lies *within* the elements of society rather than existing as some mysterious, unfathomable aberration totally outside society. Thus I think it follows that the less poverty we have in our society, the more we strive to improve everyone's status in society, the more inroads we make on criminal activity within society. Some people might disagree with this premise but I think it is a basic understanding needed in modern police practice.

Along with the ready availability of weapons, another reason for an increase in crime has been the number of civil disturbances, assassinations of public figures, and a disrespect for law generally throughout the country. Disrespect for law might be said to go back to the Revolution itself, to our Western or frontier experience, and even to our tradition in business of "grab what you can as fast as you can."

Let us remember too that disrespect for law was sustained in this country by those Southerners who held high positions in government. It was they who preached disrespect of law and counseled us to disregard the Supreme Court decisions. This is of vital importance when pondering "lawlessness" in America.

The tension, the feeling, was ultimately generated in all segments of our society: the Negro, the young, and inevitably the criminal element. I do not believe that more people have become criminals today who would not have become criminals had not civil disturbances occurred. But I do think that these disturbances, the general unrest in the country, and the blurring of legal guidelines have made those already criminal become more active and bold. I think this is true for several reasons.

First of all, they have been encouraged by the sight of large segments of the populace shouting against and acting against police and authority in general.

Second, they have realized the police were extremely busy handling these confrontations between institutions and protestors and have understood better than anyone else that the same attention and effort the police usually give to them would be, for the moment anyway, lessened. While the police are involved in keeping public order, the criminals have stepped up their illegal activity.

Third, the atmosphere engendered by the general unrest made criminals bolder. Those in the criminal group who might not have used firearms have had less reluctance to do so after seeing the leading people of the country assassinated via television.

Again, let me say that this is a matter of intensification, not of cause. Civil disorder has not transformed law-abiding citizens into criminals. It has, however, made those already outside the law feel freer in their activity. With these qualifications I think we can safely say that civil unrest and disrespect for law and order have paralleled the rise in crime.

I am perhaps surprisingly rather optimistic about the overall situation. I believe that practically all segments of society are beginning to realize where throwing brickbats at the Supreme Court and bricks at those who do not agree with us will lead. The police are now aware of the problem of poverty and of its relation to crime. We have learned much about handling civil unrest—in general we have gained much expe-

153

rience in handling all these matters and with experience comes more knowledge. Along with this will come a leveling off in crime. I think the prospects for society in the seventies look very good; for the criminal pretty bad. There is more crime, but our rate of convictions for crimes committed is steadily rising. Technology will continue to be our greatest ally in this regard.

Another problem that enters the picture at this point is what to do with the criminal once the police and the courts have identified him as a criminal. More and more we are getting away from the idea of punishment. Criminals must be sent to prison, or otherwise removed from the rest of us, for rehabilitation, not for punishment. What we must do here is make every attempt to separate first offenders from criminals. For the dismal round all too often has been this: a man goes to prison, serves his time, gets out, commits a crime, and is returned to prison. Most crimes in our society are committed by people conditioned to a life of crime. It is rare indeed for a person past twenty-five to get involved in crime if he has not been previously involved. Crime starts early; we must devote most of our efforts and attention to the first-time offender in an effort to break the vicious circle it so often follows.

Then there is middle-class crime. Shoplifting, "borrowing" supplies from the office, questionable association with people actually involved in criminal activity. Not to mention its more sophisticated abuses of privileges which are often tolerated in the business community.

The first of these is the one which gets the most attention. In the case of shoplifting it is again a case of crime following the market. People want things to the extent that they are willing to break the law. In the past shoplifting was regarded rather lightly, the improper pastime of demented old ladies. Now owners of businesses regard it as a criminal activity and

154

take all kinds of steps to prevent it. I think the best course for everyone to follow—stores, public, and police—is to regard any form of shoplifting as criminal activity and totally outside the law. No matter how minor a situation, it may possibly lead to something more serious.

A significant problem in this regard is shoplifting done by minors. Every police department must be willing to give lectures and show films at schools pointing out that shoplifting is a serious crime which carries with it penalties and often a stigma for life.

As serious a problem as shoplifting is, that of stealing by employees from employers is worse. What can employers do? They should be more alert, take every precaution, investigate a person's background carefully before he is hired for the job. Increasingly what is referred to as the "lie detector test" is being used by more and more firms to screen potential employees and reduce theft. Is this a violation of a person's rights? There is no court decision as yet. It has proved to be an effective means of reducing this type of criminal activity.

Third is the question posed by the individual who lives on the edge of crime. The shady lawyer, the unscrupulous bondsman, the "juggler," and the manipulator. These people often stay on the edge of crime and in time either operate legitimately or turn toward real crime. The number of people of this sort today I would guess is much larger than most of us would realize. Furthermore, if we accept the fact that criminal behavior is a matter of degree, then I would think it would probably be *very* large.

In terms of criminal activity, gambling probably remains the greatest problem and challenge facing the American legal system today. Society must find a way to regulate and control gambling. It is the one type of crime in which all the participants cannot be classed as criminals, as people who participate in illegal gambling activity are often law-abiding

155

citizens in all other respects. For this reason, most past attempts have failed to prohibit it. Gambling, however, should have legal guidelines set up on a national basis. At bottom, all aspects of criminal activity thrive on the money raised from gambling sources. Revenue from illegal gambling activity supports vice and prostitution. It enables a small-time thief to bankroll his operation into a large-scale enterprise. Gambling supplies cash for the expansion of criminal activity much in the way that banks supply money for legitimate business expansion. It acts as the stocks and bonds, the economic base, for all segments of criminal activity in the country.

In itself, and usually conducted as it is on a one-to-one personal basis, prostitution has little relation to major criminal activity, *except* that in large-scale criminal operations prostitution becomes part of a whole organization. Such consolidated criminal activity then becomes a major threat to lawful society. And supporting the superstructure of crime is the revenue raised by illegal gambling.

People also steal to support some type of compulsion: a demanding lover, gambling, drug addiction. A person does not usually steal for himself alone, but goes beyond the law in order to get money to support something he regards as essential to maintaining his ego, his self-esteem, or his standard of living. Most of us manage to do this through endeavors for the most part legal, but the person we classify as a criminal usually has so little confidence in himself, so little faith in what he as a personality can do, that he requires a crutch to lean upon.

Quite often, a criminal is driven by his need to impress or support a woman who more often than not is a prostitute or lives on the outer edges of society. To get her and keep her he will go far beyond the law, leading him into a deep involvement in criminal activity.

He may turn first to gambling, where in all likelihood he

will get "taken" and be forced to resort to reckless criminal activity to keep himself in kilter. The police learned long ago that whenever there is a big theft of very high-priced merchandise—diamonds, furs, the kind of goods that will bring in a great deal of money—the place to start is among the gamblers, asking who among their "clients" has recently been playing and losing heavily. This makes the gamblers nervous. A person pushed into crime to pay off gambling debts invariably brings the police to the gamblers' hangouts. Gamblers, like other groups in society, tend to gather in groups. They have favorite restaurants and other places they frequent and the police keep in touch. We have to. They are a vital source of information. They become a tool in the struggle to combat crime.

Information like this may help combat big thefts, but the true problem is left untouched—the reason for the big theft in the first place: illegal gambling activity.

Stealing to support a drug habit is a growing police problem. Drugs, once one is hooked on them, become more demanding than the desire to keep up one's status by keeping a woman or stealing to pay off gambling debts. Once a person steals to support his drug habit he is stealing because he must. The habit demands it. He has to have a "fix" and is physically compelled to get the drugs. A drug addict in search of money for a fix becomes especially dangerous. His sense of reality is blurred by the use of drugs and his individual conscience with regard to right and wrong is fuzzy. The combination of factors can drive him to steal, or just as easily to kill. It is a vexing problem. The drug addict who steals is especially dangerous because he is more likely to shoot if caught when stealing money or valuable objects than is the "routine" thief engaged in the same activity.

Probably the greatest step that could be taken by the public to help reduce all sorts of criminal activity would be to become more aware and alert to all the aspects of criminal activity within our society. It is not the single criminal act which is of the utmost importance. The number of people who have committed some kind of illegal act, whether shoplifting as a child or petty theft from an employer, is large and yet not threatening in itself.

But too frequently people can get involved in questionable activity and be up to their ears in serious crime before they know it. Again, it is not the first or the single act which is significant. It is what it can lead to. In sum, the main point I have been trying to make here is that crime should not be viewed as some awesome, dark disease existing beyond society, nor is the criminal an evil spirit marked at birth. Simply put, crime follows the market. The criminal and the citizen are in general motivated by the same desire for the good things in life that a highly industrialized society produces and advertises. At a crucial point the two types separate. One seeks things via illegal means, while the other confines his acts to legal channels. But they are both part of the basic fabric of American life.

Criminal acts cannot be separated and isolated one from the other. One cannot attack crime in bits and pieces, for if the attack is directed at one aspect alone, the criminal pollutants merely flow into other channels until the siege is lifted. The total picture must be attacked simultaneously.

Quite obviously there are no inexpensive or ready answers to cure crime. I have been in the business so long that I am at the point now where ideas of thirty years ago can be introduced as new and no one questions them. There *are* no new solutions. There is only the day-to-day effort to persuade people to adjust themselves to a legal way of living.

The profoundest thing we can say about the causes and cures of crime is that they are and have been and possibly always will be part of human existence.

9

Honesty and Sobriety

Since the beginning of modern-day local government as we know it, police power has been the vehicle to enforce the wishes of locally elected officials. But police power is a two-edged sword; when it is misused it prevents local governments from furnishing the service it was designed to furnish its citizens. Originally police services were provided by volunteers and local citizens under the supervision of a justice of the peace. This was known as the "hue and cry" system that depended on the friends and relatives of victims of crime to apprehend and prosecute perpetrators.

In 1829 Sir Robert Peel organized the Metropolitan (London) Police Force and laid the foundations on which are based all metropolitan police systems of the free world today. This was the first time a local government employed a full-time uniformed police force and accepted all the responsibilities of preventing crime by means of the arrest and prosecution of all violators. This system provided for a division of uniformed officers, or constables as they were called at the time, to patrol and to furnish a day watch and a night watch, plus a plainclothes or detective division.

It was decided that the police would wear a blue uniform —chosen by the English in order to de-emphasize police work from the military, who wore the traditional red uniform. In the beginning the police also wore the red uniform, and this caused some consternation among officialdom and the public. There was great sentiment for the police to be a strictly civilian organization and to appear so to the general public; thus the blue uniform which remains today the traditional police attire.

It was also at this time that the word "cop" came into general usage. For a long time it was thought that the word was an abbreviation for "constable on patrol" and thus a slang term not exactly complimentary to the policeman. Certainly it came to be used in this context. However, linguists now tell us that the etymology of the word "cop" comes from the Latin word *capare*, meaning "to seize or take captive." There was an Old English word *copse*, meaning "fetters," and this word also became "cops" (*Cuff* and possibly *handcuff* are derived from this root). If you accept this latter explanation then the word "cop" is a legitimate word for policeman and not, etymologically speaking, a term of disrespect. Certainly, when compared to some of the words the police have heard themselves called in the past decade, it becomes a most acceptable word for policeman.

The duties and the responsibilities of the police are designed to maintain peace and good order, to prevent crime, to protect life and property, to enforce the law, and to guarantee the freedom of the individual. The system has been expanded and updated continuously by adding specialized

160

sections such as police training, traffic control, fingerprinting, crime laboratories, crime prevention, crime commissions, and others. We still find in modern policing that the greatest deterrent to crime and the most effective crime prevention program remains the night watch and the day watch kept by qualified uniformed police officers.

The most important means necessary to a police department in successfully meeting changing conditions are police recruitment and police training. Theodore Roosevelt recognized this in 1895 when he was police commissioner of New York City and organized the first police academy, or the first police training program for a local city police department. This was probably the first attempt to bring professionalism to urban police departments. The only problem is that too little has been done since that time. The police departments that have been most successful in meeting the challenge of today are those departments with the best training programs.

For a man to have a career as an officer of the law he must possess the characteristics of honesty and sobriety. By sobriety I mean he must be sober on the job and off the job. A police officer is on duty twenty-four hours a day. All other qualities must take second place. If a person has theoretical intelligence, possesses a profound desire to aid his fellow man and a special knack or talent for police work, and does not also possess the characteristics of honesty and sobriety he cannot be an effective police officer. No matter what his intelligence, if he does not have these two qualities he and society will be far better off if he chooses some other line of work. The Atlanta Police Department has always insisted that a would-be police officer have these characteristics, for if he does not have them we cannot use him and we urge him to seek a career in another field. Insisting upon these stand-

161

ards makes it difficult to find and train police officers in to-day's society. Of course, there are a great many intelligent, honest, and sober men, but in today's affluent society they can go further in life elsewhere.

A person can be honest and upright and still fall into a trap when he becomes a police officer. A policeman must be trained to guard against the temptations placed before him and all those engaged in police work—temptations that people in other professions never have to be concerned with.

A police officer cannot be seen in public drinking beer. The police officer represents authority and must at all times be prepared to make fair and impartial decisions and cannot allow his judgment in these matters ever to be questioned. If a police officer is seen drinking in public, the word will quickly go around town that he is a lush. If he is friendly, there are those who will say he is a flirt. If he is strict, then people will shout "police brutality."

There are persons in our society who react this way toward policemen, and new policemen must be made aware of this reaction. They must not be caught off guard.

Policemen must realize from the beginning that they are always on public view, always open to inspection and criticism—just like any other part of the public domain. A man in police uniform is no longer merely a man but a symbol, and as a symbol he must learn to represent qualities over and beyond the limits of his own personality. The police officer lives in a glass house. He is a public man. Every member of the public has a part interest in him and is entitled to call upon him for aid and assistance when in trouble.

There is no such thing as an "off-duty" policeman. Think how many civil disorders and problems have been caused in recent years by the intemperate actions of supposedly off-duty policemen. A police officer may be relieved from call but he can never allow himself really to be off duty in his public personality and actions.

To instill this idea into young men who enter the police ranks as recruits the utmost care must be taken in the beginning to have the proper recruitment, training, and supervision program.

We have found that the best recruiting officer for the police force is another police officer. A well-trained, enthusiastic, dedicated police officer can do more to attract other qualified men to become police officers than anyone else. He cannot do enough, though. Our highly competitive society has made it difficult to find good men in all fields, and this is doubly true in recruiting people for police work. In recent years we have tried out several types of programs to improve the recruitment of good officers. We send our people throughout the state talking to school groups, giving interviews—going into small towns and the rural sections of the state looking for people.

We also recruit out of state. We have been allowed to hire aliens if we are unable to fill vacancies from the citizen population. We have on the police force men who are Irish, German, and Scots aliens who are doing outstanding jobs as police officers. We make every effort to find people who we think would make good officers. We seek them all the time; we do not sit around hoping they will come to us.

Our standards are tough. We state that a person must be a high school graduate. In recent years we have not held to this rule in all cases. If a person is not a high school graduate but can pass a specially devised personnel department test, he may be hired. I wish to make clear that this matter has to be decided on an individual basis, each case examined carefully and decided on the basis of the individual involved.

If a person cannot pass the test or is not a high school graduate then he cannot pass in the police training school. If we do find a person of good character in this category, we can employ him in another capacity as a guard—something like a teacher's aide or nurse's aide—while he continues his education and qualifies to become a police officer.

The person who wants to become a policeman cannot have a police record. Nor will we hire a man who has been a juvenile offender. Such people can work as guards or as community service officers, but they may not be police officers.

Health standards are very high, well above those required for induction into the army. A police officer must be healthy and in reasonably good condition. The tests in the police training school require a person of intelligence to pass them, while the agility test requires that a person be in good physical condition.

If the recruit gets this far he still must remain on a six-month probationary period before he can have full status. During this six-month period he is observed closely and if found not to be adapted to police work we must release him. This is best for the department and for the individual.

The prospective police officer must also undergo a strenuous character investigation. Fingerprints can be checked with the FBI, including a file on criminal fingerprints anywhere in the Western world. We talk to the people in the neighborhood where the individual lived from the age of ten upward.

We also contact all past employers. If the person is from out of the area we get in touch with law-enforcement officials in the area he is from. What does that police department know about the candidate? Was he in trouble as a youth? We also request high school records. If the character investigation turns up nothing in the person's background that would keep him from being a good police officer, he then has to undergo an oral interview.

It is the task of a police department to talk with and interview people constantly. It is our business. Thus, when a new man comes in for his interview he talks with an experienced police officer who has the knowledge and know-how to find out pretty quickly if the person is truthful and honest. If there is any suspicion on our part the candidate must waive the right for us to examine his juvenile or military records. If he is truthful he will have no objection to furnishing us with the necessary records.

The new recruit, having successfully passed all these hurdles, is now ready to become a police officer. He is sworn in, given the oath, and placed on duty. He will go immediately to work for a period of four to six months with the Crime Prevention Bureau. Here he will find out firsthand what life is like for those people who did not grow up in his kind of neighborhood and are not exposed to the same background or culture. This is really a period of education and psychological stretching for the new officer. He will be working in poor neighborhoods, finding out what goes on in the various community centers in those areas, learning the problems of people living in high crime neighborhoods.

If the new recruit is repelled by any of this, if he does not relate to the people living there, and if after this period of duty with Crime Prevention he shows hostility toward the problem, then it is certainly better for him and for the department to find it out early.

In practically all cases this period when the new recruit works in CP is the most valuable of his training period. He completes his duty there full of questions concerning operations and functions of the police in a modern society. We put him in CP duty first because in this day it is essential for him to have this experience.

From this point the recruit goes through the Atlanta Police

Academy. This school lasts for seven weeks. While the recruit is in school his entire time is spent there with eight hours of classes. The recruit studies such subjects as:

Authority of Police Officers
Duties and Responsibilities
History of Police Work
Rules and Regulations
Rules of Evidence
Patrol Methods
Investigations and Reports

The instructors in the school are generally very experienced police personnel in their own fields. We also bring in outside people who have something special to contribute. As an example, the Rev. Sam Williams, professor at Morehouse College, and an official of the Southern Christian Leadership Conference, has for many years been a speaker on race relations.

We try to stress over and over again the special problems policemen are subject to which do not confront people in other types of work. The rookie policeman is told time and time again that he is *responsible* for his *actions.* It is also stressed that he will be held strictly accountable for any actions he takes that are not justifiable by the rules and regulations of the department.

The rookie policeman studies actual cases and acts out actual court cases in which members of the class assume various roles as members of the court. Is the evidence presented good enough? Did the policeman make a proper investigation at the scene? Every effort is made to make the case study as realistic as possible.

As an example of these problems, a woman called me recently to say how outraged she was over an incident involving an injured man and the police. When the policeman

166

arrived on the scene he took the injured man's watch, ring, and billfold. She was incensed that an injured person should be thus robbed by the police!

This was of course not at all the case. The policeman was merely taking the person's valuables for protection, placing a "hold" on them at the police station until the victim or a relative could claim them. This is standard police procedure, but the lady who saw it was unaware of this and had leaped to an erroneous conclusion. This shows the necessity for police officers to understand the need to explain their actions to the public and not to become indignant if falsely accused by a citizen of improper behavior.

One of our most serious problems involves losing good policemen. A new man may come into the department, go through all the tests, interviews, and training and after about two years' service leave the department for a better-paying job elsewhere. The reason most often given for leaving is that a man grows weary of the thankless job he is asked to perform. Public misunderstanding of the police role and police function is also usually cited as making the job difficult and finally impossible. Another common cause of resignation may be that the wife or mother or some other relative has become weary of the dangers and insults the policeman is confronted with daily and insists that he get into some other kind of work. There is a special burden which wives and members of policemen's families must carry. Like the officer, they also live in a glass house and must be able to make the adjustment. I have often thought it would be a good idea to have some kind of orientation course for policemen's wives to become acquainted more fully with police work. They need to understand that they often bring anguish to themselves by actions that are misunderstood by the public. What I am saying is that a policeman's wife must realize that her husband's job is different, that its duties and responsibilities involve every

167

part of him, and that police work is not a nine-to-five operation.

We must also stress to the new police officer that nowadays the demands made upon him by the public are greater than ever before. People are more aware of what their rights are and their demands follow accordingly. The policeman must keep himself informed and alert. There will be those who will try to influence him, to gain preferential treatment. Some will offer to buy him a drink, thereby compromising his position in a public place. The rookie must learn all of this in his training period or else he will be inadequately prepared to do his police duty.

One question often arises during this period of training: How much authority does a policeman possess and how much force is he allowed to exercise in the performance of his duty? Not until the very last period of his training does an officer become involved with firearms. An awesome responsibility rests on the shoulders of a policeman in the use of a firearm. More often than not the police officer will have only a split second in which to make the right judgment in firing his weapon. He will not make that right decision until he has been properly trained in the handling and use of firearms and until he has been made fully aware of the conditions under which he may use his firearm.

The well-trained policeman will display restraint and scrupulously avoid the indiscriminate use of his firearm. He will shoot only as a very last resort. There are two things which every police officer must consider before he fires his gun. First, he must be sure that he is legally entitled to fire his weapon in this particular instance. Second, he must be sure his use of the firearm does not violate departmental regulations, which could cost him his job.

These rules of the Atlanta Police Department allow an officer to use his weapon in defense of his own life or the lives of others. A policeman may fire his weapon at an escaping

168

felon (that is, barring some new legal judgment in this regard), but not at a thirteen-year-old who has just taken a shirt out of a window broken by someone else. However, suppose he fires his gun at a person he thinks is an escaping felon and who turns out not to be?

The department investigates every wounding or killing of a person by a policeman exactly as any other shooting. Do the facts justify the shooting? Was the policeman using poor judgment? Homicide detectives investigate the shooting to determine any criminal liability. The Police Department's internal security division checks the case for violations of departmental rules. It is departmental policy to investigate the shooting first and then forward all facts to the grand jury and the district attorney's office for their attention. If it is a serious case of a policeman unlawfully using his gun, the grand jury can make its own investigation and take whatever action it deems appropriate. It is important to have an independent agency involved in these matters because in this way it never appears that the police are attempting to cover anything up.

There are occasions when a policeman will be forced to shoot someone. In the overwhelming majority of cases, policemen fire guns only in self-defense or to protect the lives of others. When this is not the case, the procedural and investigative machinery is set in motion. All the facts are gathered and made available to all parties concerned. Every effort is made to keep the public aware of all such cases and to cover nothing up. In fact, police activity must be public record at all times.

To avoid any tragedies of this nature, rookies on the Atlanta police force are not issued firearms until after completing their initial training with the CP Bureau. Only then is the new policeman issued a firearm. Then he reports to the Georgia Police Academy for eighty hours of classroom instruction on various operating procedures and the correct use of firearms, including target practice.

When a police recruit finishes his training at the Police Academy he is assigned to work with another officer until he is ready for permanent assignment. During this period he is carefully guided in the ways of good police practice. The new policeman will ultimately be patrolling in a one-man patrol car. To provide good police service and the necessary coverage and patrol, the Atlanta Police Department has adopted one-man patrol cars. This has been a highly controversial subject and has brought me much criticism from within and without the department. This is a subject that is unfortunately often misunderstood and emotionally considered. When a police officer is injured or killed in the line of duty, the practice naturally receives a great deal of publicity, and there are those who sincerely believe the incident would have been prevented by the use of a two-man patrol car. The facts simply do not support this assumption.

The department adopted one-man patrol cars for the following reasons:

1. The record, both local and national, shows that more police officers are killed in two-man than in one-man patrol cars.

2. A majority of the calls answered by the police do not require any action by them—merely counseling, giving of advice.

3. When a police officer needs to call for assistance he has twice the number of units to call on and can get help faster than he could otherwise.

4. Sound police management requires an officer to do his own thinking, to use his own initiative and imagination, and to develop so that each day he does a better job.

5. For the Atlanta police to adopt arbitrarily the two-man patrol car would cause the number of patrol units and the police service to be cut in half, or it would require all police

personnel to work seven days per week, instead of five days.

What it all amounts to is that two-man patrol cars became a luxury we could no longer afford, or rather one that the taxpayers were unwilling to finance. To overcome these handicaps the city is constantly striving to add more police and to increase police compensation and fringe benefits, but again this will make police services extremely expensive for the taxpayer.

At this point the rookie in his patrol car is now a full-fledged patrolman, but his training is far from complete. He will return to the Police Academy at various times during his career to study new police methods and review past practices. All Atlanta police officers attend the Georgia Police Academy run by the state. Many go to the FBI Academy in Washington for further study. Fourteen of our officers have completed courses at the Academy. Several have attended the Traffic Institute at Northwestern University and many more the Southern Police Institute at Louisville, Kentucky, (Robert W. Woodruff contributes five scholarships a year for members of the Atlantic Police Department to attend the Southern Police Institute.) A number of our police personnel have earned their college diplomas. Forty-eight officers now attend colleges and universities in the Atlanta area, completing courses of instruction in their off-duty hours. Thirty-three of our officers are holders of bachelors' degrees and eight have masters' degrees in law. Thirteen officers hold other various degrees including one bachelor of divinity. In recent years one of the most important subjects taught to the new police recruit is the subject of "how to recognize and deal with people with mental health problems." We have volunteers from the local mental health field for this purpose. A policeman's training and schooling can never end.

In order to keep the police departments of the nation staffed with qualified, well-trained officers, certain incentives

171

of salary and professional standing must be added in the future. For too long we have been losing good men because the rate of increase in police pay has not kept pace with other governmental and business positions. Policemen who have the drive and incentive to get one to four years of college education must be paid in accordance with the higher qualifications earned through extended education.

Better pay is only part of the answer, however. Most problems in police departments do not center around money. At the time of the Detroit riot in 1967, the officers in the department were the highest paid in the nation, yet, as the Riot Commission found, good police pay does not of itself lead to better police practice. Two weeks before the Detroit riot the police organization within the department had called a "blue Monday" when police officers called in sick for a day to protest working conditions in the department. So-called blue Mondays have been a problem in many police departments since that time. Many factors contribute to the phenomenon.

Since the beginning of the civil rights revolution of the sixties more and more has been asked of, even demanded of, our policemen. We require police officers to be more energetic, more alert, and more responsive to the needs and desires of people and to be ready to provide intelligent police service. Today it is not enough to tell a man to go out and patrol and keep the peace and good order. The day when the big cop on the corner could enforce public behavior with a billy club is gone with the wind. We now require our policemen to think, reflect, and reach enlightened decisions on the basis of what is happening in the world today. The policeman is better educated, and the kind of department and working conditions that satisfied the policeman of twenty-five years ago are unsatisfactory to the man in blue today. Everything else in the world is changing. Why not the conditions around the old station house?

172

The "blue flu," or the "blue revolution," is but an extension of the civil rights revolution or the bringing of this revolution to focus on the policeman's working conditions, just as it came to focus upon conditions on college campuses. If other groups in society can gain their ends through confrontations and strikes, applying pressure on authority to bring about change, the police officer who has been the man in the middle of all this change now wonders why the same pressure cannot be applied on his own behalf. In so far as this protest brings about more up-to-date police practice, better working conditions, and better pay for the police, it is to the good of both public and police.

But in most cases this situation is exactly the opposite. The blue protest within police departments is usually led by those who wish to go against the trends of the day, to abolish the revolution of the sixties and return police practice to what it was twenty or thirty years ago. They are against the courts, the Negroes, all minority groups, and everybody not in accord with what their thinking about an American ought to be. They want to keep police departments lily white and do not want to see the police involved in any way with the problems of poverty in urban life.

Whether these groups are police unions or masqueraders under the title of Fraternal Order of Police, they represent the worst in policing and are a continuing threat to modern police practice in this nation. The public must be made quickly aware of this problem and must demand that their policemen belong to no organizations seeking to step backward into the past. The disgruntled must be shown by a responsive public that there is no place in America for their kind of racist philosophy.

The national organization of the Fraternal Order of Police has grown in recent years. Police unions have also grown in membership and expanded and in some areas even gained recognition from the American Federation of Labor. This activity may result in the creation of dangerous counterforces within police departments, yet no other group is doing anything about police pay and police working conditions. Police join these groups because in part society forces them to do so. The city of Atlanta has given its policemen pay raises, attempted to upgrade their working conditions, and has actively supported all national legislation to assist local police departments.

The big problem in the whole country is that generally those in the Congress and in the population who scream the loudest for law and order are those who have been mute for years and have done nothing to alter conditions that would truly help create law and order—by the upgrading of local police departments.

I look forward to the day when the U.S. Justice Department and the U.S. Congress will say to every city police department, regardless of its size: "If your department meets all the professional standards in police recruitment, police pay, police training, and police supervision, the federal government will contribute to your annual budget." It should certainly be in the neighborhood of 50 percent.

The great objection to this, other than the plea that there are higher priorities for the use of federal funds, is the nineteenth-century insistence of doing things in the old way with no interference from anyone. Everyone objects to federal guidelines necessary to qualify for federal money, yet the Supreme Court in the past decade has set down the most stringent guidelines ever placed upon the local police departments of this nation. The guidelines are there, in the decisions in cases I have already considered: Mapp, Escobedo, Miranda, *et al.*

Turning federal money over to the states will be about as effective as dropping it in a rain barrel. The states do not have these problems and have had no practice in handling them. The problem of America is the problem of the cities. It is our most pressing problem and must be met—and quickly.

When I insist that local police departments must receive federal funds I am often accused of advocating a federal police force. Well, I do not advocate a federal police force, but the mere thought of one does not frighten me as much as do the activities of the Fraternal Order of Police, to cite one example. The Fraternal Order of Police was organized many years ago as a fraternity for the police. It started as a strictly social organization, but in my opinion it now appears to be a substitute for a police union. Police unions have been discredited or outlawed in many places.

The Atlanta Police Department devotes most of its time and effort to enforcing state and federal laws, rather than city ordinances. To enforce federal laws it is necessary to accept a certain amount of federal control and to follow federal procedures. We have reached the point in our city affairs where we no longer really have any choice in the matter. The time has come when the best efforts and resources of the federal, state, and local governments are required to meet the high cost of law enforcement and to check and reverse the trend of increasing crime that we have experienced in recent years.

The biggest problem that I have had to surmount in my career has been that of race. It has been a part of our past and will be a part of our future whether it centers around the Negro or some other racial minority. Independent of race, the problem of the disadvantaged in our society will also continue. The segment of society most continually in contact with these groups will be the police. The police must obviously be trained to this special job. The Georgia State College in Atlanta now offers a two-year course in Police Administration which leads to an associate of arts degree. Twenty-six

Atlanta police officers are presently enrolled in this program. We are justly proud of this college as it is one of the few institutions in the nation offering this course. We would hope that more colleges across the nation would offer courses in police work.

The police in our society are often resented because they represent authority, an authority much too often abused. This country was founded by people fleeing from oppressive authority. To be free of authority the Constitution was written with numerous built-in safeguards and was to be the basis of a fair and judicial authority. We now see that these safeguards were insufficient to protect a sizable portion of the population from oppression by overt authority. All the turmoil of the sixties was but an enraged protest against blind authority.

The police in America have had a strange history. The inherited fear of authority has resulted in an indiscriminate urge to keep the police down. Until the past two decades of this century the police image was one to inspire only weak sentimentality and ridicule. Since the invention of the motion picture the portrayal of the policeman as a bungling nincompoop has been one of the essential messages of that art form. If authority can be laughed at it cannot hurt you. Who can forget Charlie Chaplin as the ridiculous dictator with the funny mustache? No one should ever forget.

What we need in the future are policemen who are neither feared nor laughed at. We need policemen who represent the law and support justice in a democratic society. This new breed of policeman is already in the middle stages of development but to bring him to maturity will require the determined will of society to change its attitude and supply the moral and financial support.

If this new will also is manifested on society's part in providing the disadvantaged not only with a new breed of police

176

officer but also with a new kind of education and a new kind of environment in which to live, then the great social revolution of our time will be the first to come about without serious bloodshed.

From what I have seen in the past I am very hopeful about the future. I think that American society, particularly Southern American society, has moderated its attitude and changed for the better more than any society in the same period of time in the annals of history. I am inclined to feel quite confident of the future.

When we get there, however, we will encounter new problems. The second most vexing problem in my police career has been that caused by the automobile. Since its introduction into American life more violence and mayhem have occurred on the highways and streets of America than has been committed on the battlefields or in hundreds of civil disorders. How many families in America have been touched by loss of life and property in automobile accidents?

As our population expands during the last part of the century the congestion caused by the automobile will bring about a kind of paralysis of movement. Then it will become a police problem to try to persuade the mobile American citizen that he cannot drive his automobile anywhere, anytime, and anyplace he pleases. No doubt restrictions will be necessary and people will have to divide their mobility between some form of mass transit and private car travel under specific regulations, but the American citizen has cherished his "rights" to his automobile almost as much as he has cherished his prejudices. It will be as big a job getting him to modify the former as it was the latter.

A casual approach toward the law will no doubt be a characteristic of the future. All institutions, including home, church, family, democracy, and almost any you can think of, have suffered terrible blows. Where we once acquiesced rev-

erently we now ask, will it work? Since the coming generations will be pragmatists above everything else, the future
policeman must be guided not by how it was done in the past
but how it will work in the world of the future.

Thus emerges the picture of a new breed of policeman.
The man who wears two hats—one of toughness and the
other of tolerance. An officer who respects the law but is also
capable of bearing the spirit, not the letter alone. We need
a man who is the result of training given by policemen before
him who did their job well. I suspect the police officer in
years ahead will have more respect and hold a higher position in society than any of his forebears.

10

The Continuing Reappraisal

Many questions remain unanswered. In recent months the police have been "discovered." Some even speak of our time as the decade or age of the policeman. Why has so much attention been focused on the police? What has brought the man in blue into the limelight? There remain many questions but few answers.

What is the policeman's role today? Protection for the people or control of them?

The role or function of the police officer in present-day life is constantly being re-examined. The question of whether or not the policeman's role has changed is redundant. Those of us with responsibilities in this field know full well that it has changed, and radically. The reasons for this are complex.

The Supreme Court decisions, the black revolution, the protests of Americans young and old against the Vietnam

179

War, the upheavals within the nation's high schools, colleges, and universities, and the awareness of the American people generally with regard to their rights and their relations with the police—all these elements, brought about by advances in education and the communication media, have focused attention on the question of people and police. As a result, many people are confused about the role of the police officer in America today. Is he to control people or to protect them? The answer must be "both."

The policeman is the symbol of the law. He represents to each of us the authority of a freely chosen democratic government. Even a democratic government, in order to exist, must rest on certain rules and regulations that all of us must obey. Those who do not obey these laws come more readily into contact with the police. If our society was unchanging and authoritarian, the issue would be clear-cut and there would arise few of the problems that beset the police officer in a free society.

A democratic society means a changing society. In one situation the police might be in the position of protecting people but, because our society changes, attitudes and interpretations will change and what was protection in the past turns out to be containment in the future. Or the other way around.

It is possible these days that the police may be called on to control a group that only recently was protected. Suppose the police are at the scene of a large peace demonstration within a park area of a large city. It is an orderly protest for peace. The group has obtained permission from city authorities to hold the meeting and to parade through certain streets following the meeting. During the parade certain persons in direct opposition to the peace movement abuse the demonstrators by throwing rocks at them. The police move in quickly to put a stop to this. They are there to protect the demonstrators, whose legal rights are sound.

Suppose a day later this same group gathers on a college campus to protest without authorization. The same academic people who would have criticized the police had they not protected the peace demonstrators now demand that these demonstrators be removed from the campus by the police. It often turns out to be true that those who are most critical of police methods may eventually demand that the police use those same methods should rioting or protest erupt in their own back yards.

In the 1963 confrontation in Birmingham between the police, led by Bull Connor, and the civil rights marchers, led by Martin Luther King, were the police attempting to protect or control the crowds? Obviously they were trying to control the citizens, using whatever means or force was necessary to keep down the civil rights revolution. The police in Birmingham in 1963 were criticized by all civilized people throughout the world. The tactics used were so severe that it ultimately led to the passage of the Civil Rights Act of 1964. The police in this instance, as in all such confrontations, played a large role in the final achievement of the aims of all the protest movements. In these cases the rough tactics used by the Birmingham police—dogs, water hoses, cattle prods, etc.—helped defeat the police purpose. Americans are above all a fair people. From the news media they could see how unfair these methods were. This created a vast wave of sympathy for the oppressed.

The role of the policeman of *itself* has had influence on the direction or course of events. When people realized this they became interested in taking a long hard look at the police function. By their actions in controlling protesters the police have usually helped the protesters; ultimately those seeking change are encouraged to provoke the police, certainly if they can do so in full view of the television cameras.

When in 1963 the Atlanta police refused to enforce segregation laws once the courts had ruled other such laws illegal, we were accused of being too protective of protesters and disrupters. In this instance the demonstrations were peaceful until those who felt the police were being too lenient tried to take matters into their own hands and do a little containing on their own. The police cannot follow their own ideas or a citizen's of what the law should be. In a democratic society they can only follow what the courts say the law is.

The police offered protection (in the guise of the U.S. Army) to a member of the civil rights revolution, James Meredith, when he entered the University of Mississippi in 1962. But in 1968 the police attempted to control the student protesters at Columbia University. In both cases the presence of the police was offensive to most academic people. Whenever the police enter a school, college, or university campus they do so because the preceding policies have led to total failure. Nobody in his right mind wants to see the police battling with the students on college campuses. I insist most strongly that this is *not* a police function.

In many protests today the leadership of the university or institution involved is saying in effect: "Everything else has failed, let's call in the cops." If I were to get a call such as this my reply would be: "You made the mess. Get in there and straighten it out. Don't be calling on the police to bail you out. This is not a police function." Or at least I would feel like saying that.

Conflicts between student protesters and college officials come about for the same reason that conflicts come about between demonstrators and police. The police would still be battling the civil rights revolution in the streets had we not become involved with the causes that led to this protest.

All the protest of the time is basically a protest against authority. It is a protest against the symbols of authority:

182

parents, teachers, and the police. What the protesters are in effect saying is that they will no longer accept authority simply because it is authority. They will accept only authority that is not unreasonable and is involved with serious problems of society. Much more is involved than protests vs. authority. They are the conditions of life—war, poverty, racism—which are the underlying causes of discontent. As representing the ultimate authority, when do police become involved and not involved in these protests?

Police become involved when order ceases to exist. Violence is not directed against a puff of smoke, but is directed *toward* something—most often authority—or merely against those with a different point of view. Where the police make a grave error is in allowing themselves to become the patsy in the situation; that is, in allowing themselves to become the *object* of the protest. What begins as a confrontation at a university between students and administration often ends up as a battle between students and police. The college or university is not doing its job or the confrontation would never erupt. Likewise, the police are not on their toes or they would not allow themselves to be maneuvered into the position of taking the brunt of the protest. The police must keep order but they must do so without becoming a party to the protest. This is not their proper role.

How should the police react during these disturbances? First of all, they should not rush into a situation without careful thought and planning. They should go in not with the idea of controlling people but of offering police protection to all those involved wherever needed. Second, they should go in with sufficiently well-trained policemen who can separate "eyeballers" (onlookers) from the leaders among the protesters. These latter should be arrested if necessary and removed from the scene. This can be done without major upheavals. Third, there should be extensive follow-up and investigation

183

on those arrested and strong cases taken into court against them. Without this planning and clear understanding with officials the police would be well advised never to enter a university prior to the committing of violence. The mere occupying of a building by protesters is not violence. Violence occurs only when the police begin moving them out. The police officer's role in today's time of protest is to be a referee. The police are not protesting and they commit a grave error if by intention or force of circumstance they become involved in the protest.

The policeman has great influence on the forces of change within our society. The particular attitude of a particular officer, the particular stance he assumes, can often influence the course of events. By being more tolerant than hard-nosed against those in protest he can be more effective and contribute to the good order of the community. He can help society change with as little violence as possible. Certainly not everyone will agree with this position—and I have the scars from past experience to prove it. But I still insist it is not a police function to become a participant in any confrontation.

Are there any new methods to improve police practice?

In spite of all we hear about advances in the use of new equipment and scientific analysis, the police are just beginning to scratch the surface in the use of technology in fighting crime. I look forward in the next few years to some real breakthroughs in developing new technological means to combat crime.

In the area of crime reporting and the keeping of records we have already witnessed a tremendous advance. One of the reasons, but assuredly not the only reason, for a higher crime rate in America today is the improved methods of reporting criminal activity. In the past the police did not give

184

as much attention to this aspect of police work. Now all crimes become case studies for research and analysis.

Some years ago I noticed a great increase in the number of rapes of Negro women by Negro men reflected in the crime reports. Following a careful study of the cases, the department concluded that the rate of increase was occurring in a particular area because it was being reported more often. In the past the rape of a Negro woman by a Negro man was too often not a serious police concern. If a report was made, it was treated lightly. (If this is not an example of the white racism which the Riot Commission referred to, I don't know what is.) When the members of the Negro community realized that the police were becoming aware of this situation and beginning to do something about the reports when made, they began to report the cases whenever they took place. There was no rate of increase in the actual crime, merely a rate of increase in the reporting of the crime. With better record keeping and the use of computers this is true to a lesser extent of all crimes.

The organization which is doing the best job in the field of research and development is the International Association of Chiefs of Police. For many years this organization was little more than a social group of chiefs of police. However, as demands for police service and changes in police functions began accelerating, many of us in the IACP felt the organization should be more than a social group. Under the direction of its capable and energetic executive director, Quinn Tamm, the IACP over the past decade has become the most effective organization in the world dedicated to crime reduction and improving police departments. Under its leadership and guidance many police departments in this country have been able to emerge from the dark ages of law enforcement into the twentieth century. In all its good works the IACP has made no greater contribution to good law enforcement than

185

in the field of research and development.

The IACP maintains a facility unique in the police service, a Center for Law Enforcement Research Information. A continuous flow of material from individuals, foundations, colleges, industry, and police departments comes into this center and is disseminated throughout the IACP membership. Progressive methods developed in one police department can thus be utilized by other departments. The IACP also provides a managerial consultant service for all member departments. The IACP has a permanent staff of some ten veteran police executives with academic training through the master's degree level in its Field Operations Division. At the request of a community, local crime commission, mayor, or chief of police, this division may conduct a detailed analysis of the police department's administration and operations. Based on this analysis, recommendations are made to increase its efficiency. Over a hundred law-enforcement agencies throughout the country have made use of this service.

The activity of the IACP and all other groups in the field of research and development must be speeded up. This, along with training, is the answer for improving law enforcement in the future.

Should a citizen report all crimes to the police?

Some people have the feeling that there is very little the police can do and there is no need to report some crimes. Maybe I am being "too much the policeman," but I feel that if a person does not report a crime, no matter how minor or seemingly insignificant, he is trying to hide something rather than being just lazy or indifferent. I find it inconceivable that a citizen who is robbed, assaulted, or burglarized will not report it to the police unless he has something to conceal.

186

Even if only items of small value are taken from the home it should be reported to the police. Individual criminal activity against one citizen is part of a larger pattern of criminal activity. Maybe in a particular case the amount stolen is not large, maybe the location or the type of article taken is of importance and is an essential piece of the police puzzle in bringing criminals to justice. No matter how insignificant—report it. Only the police can determine the true significance of any particular crime.

Does the use of Mace or other similar products aid the police in controlling civil disorders?

The only way to control an outbreak of smallpox is to inoculate people. The only way to control civil disorders is to prevent them. All the so-called new products being churned out by industry and sold to local governments to control rioting are of no value. They are primarily attempts by some to find a cheap way of combating police problems in the present day. There is no cheap way. There are no ready answers. If local governments would put the money into good crime-prevention programs that they put into such things as Mace and Pepper Fog and other "armaments" they would be getting more for their money and would lessen the likelihood of rioting and street disorders.

Of course the idea behind Mace and other such products is to control people without shooting them. On the face of it, this sounds like a good idea, but the end result will be the abolishment of police departments to let the army deal with such problems. This is no answer to the problem. The civilian population is not an enemy. Any attempts by the police to use such things as Mace against large segments of the population place the police in a military posture. The use of tear gas does

187

the same thing. Tear gas should never be used against civilians; it should only be used against individual criminals to protect policemen: that is, if a person is barricaded within a building and is shooting at the people or the police. The assumption by the police of a military posture in a democratic society will always get the police in trouble. Thank goodness.

Would it contribute to improved law enforcement if the policemen on the beat were disarmed?

This policy is followed in some Western European countries. It would be a good policy to follow in the United States, but with one major corollary—and it is certainly a most important one. The civilian population must be disarmed at the same time. There are 200 million firearms in private hands in America. This means that proportionately the citizen community has as many guns as the police! The primary need for arming the police is to protect them from the people in the population who have guns. In my view both should be disarmed.

It has been my observation that the primary difference between police enforcement in America and police enforcement in most other Western nations is that in minor offenses of the law the police there might be considered more tolerant, and if not tolerant certainly less concerned. As long as a situation does not get out of hand it is a general police policy not to become involved. But if the situation does become intense or if the crime is a serious one, the police response is harsher than here.

I believe, however, if the interest shown by foreign police departments in our methods of crime prevention is any indication, the situation in other countries is changing fast.

188

What is the function of the lower courts in this time of social revolution?

The greatest weakness in our court system has been the failure of the lower courts, in all too many instances, to understand and execute decisions of the Supreme Court. We need more young lawyers involved in the court system. Not enough money is being spent to attract young people, and there are too many part-time judges. There are millions of cases in the lower courts and few on the Supreme Court level. Every case brought into these courts of first instance must not just be "another case" to the police and the courts. For the individual involved his case is one of the most important things to occur in his whole life. If the police and the courts do not follow Supreme Court guidelines, the individual involved may well become a court casualty. Miranda and Escobedo were court casualties. We cannot afford any more. Every case must stand on its own merits and the penalty imposed must be in accordance with the facts, depending on the discretion, competence, and integrity of the lower court which first hears every individual case.

Is crime in America really skyrocketing?

In 1967 Atlanta had a 23.3 percent increase in major crimes. This is more than twice the increase in industry and population for the same period in Atlanta. *Yes,* crime is increasing faster than we are.

While the increase in crime was up 23.3 percent, there was a 26 percent increase in the number of indictments. We hear a great deal about the increasing crime rate but very little about the increase in number of arrests. We also do not hear enough about the fact that 35 percent of all persons arrested for major crimes are under seventeen years of age. Who is responsible for this? Do we blame police, parents, society in general, or disrespect for law in today's society? At the same time, we do not hear enough about the high percentage of repeat arrests. Again, do we blame our police, our prisons, or our social agencies for failing to do a good job of rehabilitation? Actually, of course, simply seeking to ascribe the blame for our rising crime rate leads us nowhere. But we can emphasize once more the three significant points concerning this increase.

1. Our crime rate is higher than ever, but our arrest and conviction rate is just as high, and in most areas higher.

From this we may conclude that certainty of punishment is not the deterrent to crime that it once was thought to be. More crimes are being committed but fewer are left unsolved than in the past. So, in spite of all the criticism directed at the Supreme Court, criminals are not running around scot-free. But it seems clear that people are not intimidated by threat of punishment to the extent they once were. How are we to deal with this? Mete out stiffer penalties? This is but a short-term answer.

2. The rate of major crimes committed by persons under seventeen years of age is rising faster than the over-all crime rate.

This, in essence, means that much of the increase in crime in America can be attributed to children! Amazingly, we are not speaking here about petty offenses, but major crimes involving force and violence.

There are two answers to this aspect of the crime problem. Both are expensive. First of all, we must stop sending first offenders to prison. This is as barbaric as capital punishment, if not more so. We must make a stronger effort to keep minors from becoming habitual criminals.

Second, we must increase our efforts in crime prevention.

The whole crime-prevention program is primarily aimed at this age group. Thus far we have made only a small dent in the problem. It does no good to lambast parents or churches or society in general for not doing their jobs. This will not solve the problem. The solution lies with the immediate involvement of the federal government in a broad program of crime prevention. Let us stop arguing about "guidelines" and controls and priorities. After the race issue, this is the number-one problem facing the federal government today. The children of America are our greatest resource, but we are shamefully neglecting them. To continue to do so can place the entire nation in the greatest peril. Local police departments need to be spending an amount equal to their present budgets on crime prevention alone. The money must come from the federal government as the problem is nationwide in character and importance.

3. Most crimes are committed by repeaters.

We are doing little in the field of rehabilitation. If a person has more than two arrests, or is sent up for the second time, he receives practically nothing in the way of rehabilitation.

The answer to this problem is simple. Solve problem number two, that is, do something about serious juvenile crime, and this problem will vanish, for it exists because of the failure to do anything about crimes committed by those under seventeen years of age.

When one begins talking about the skyrocketing crime rate inevitably more questions are raised than answered. The only answer the police have been able to devise is crime prevention. Maybe an intensified crime-prevention program on the national level would of itself generate more answers.

What can be done about widespread corruption in the police force?

A more appropriate question would be: what can the police force do about the widespread corruption in society? I believe that probably the least corrupt person in America today is the police officer. If this were not the case he would not have such difficulty understanding why so many people among the youth and the minorities of America will not obey the law. The police obey the law zealously. They ask, why won't everyone else?

Certainly in the past graft and corruption on the police force were a major problem, but I do not think it is a problem of any significance today. It is no longer a major problem because today the police are closely scrutinized. If a policeman is dishonest, the press, his neighbors, his fellow officers, the public will know about it real quick. There is a fierce and growing pride among the new breed of policemen. Where once a police officer might take a bribe, he now looks upon the person offering such a bribe with contempt. How can this complete turnaround in attitude be explained?

It has been a part of American folklore to look upon the policeman with derision. If he made mistakes he was laughed at. If he could not be laughed at he was accused of dishonesty. Policemen came in two categories: those who were honest because they were too dumb to be otherwise; a smart policeman was a rich policeman. What person in any other profession would be accused of dishonesty if he bought a new car or a new house? The acquiring of almost anything left the policeman wide open to the charge of dishonesty. If he was not dishonest, he was using his job for his own personal gain. To be a policeman meant you had to be poor. Society would not tolerate it otherwise. Keeping the policeman poor left him vulnerable and open to temptation, made him an easy target for bribery. If one police officer was so bribed, then the entire police force was open to the charge. J. Edgar Hoover realized this as the major problem in running an effective law-enforcement organization. Members of the FBI are the highest-paid enforcement officers in the world.

Why did society tolerate this situation for so long? The answer, as I have indicated previously, lies within all of us: our peculiarly American fear of authority. This country was founded by people fleeing authority. They wanted to escape from a feared authoritarian society. We as present-day Americans have inherited this fear. But as long as the closest symbol of authority—the cop—can be laughed at or thought dishonest it cannot threaten us or hurt us.

There are still those who insist that crime in America would not be what it is if we could just have honest policemen. Honest police officers would ferret out the wrongdoers, and the crime problem would diminish. This attitude ignores the real problem and is a refusal to see our society as it is.

I think the press in this country, particularly the local press, is guilty of such an attitude. Like all of us, the press is caught up in its own folklore. Too much energy is expended in looking for "bad apples" in the police barrel. The modern methods of recruitment, training, and supervision eliminate 99 percent of the people who would not make good police officers. The press would do far better to berate police departments for their lack of involvement in crime prevention and their rigidities toward the problems of the present day. To do otherwise is simply a refusal to face up to reality.

I do not think that crime arises from lack of honesty among policemen or some dark force outside society. There is no source of the conspiracy because I do not believe there is a conspiracy. Crime is the result, or by-product, of our society. If it cannot be cured, certainly it can be treated.

What can the police do about drug use?

Any action that tends to reduce drug abuse. There is, of course, a very definite pattern between drug use and crime. The drug user needs money to support his very expensive habit. There are those who argue that if certain drugs were legalized, this would reduce crime. I strongly doubt it. In one sense the use of dangerous drugs is similar to a criminal act: it is not the first or single act that leads to trouble, but the pattern which is established. If the use of drugs began and ended with "bennies" or "pep pills," legalization might be the answer. But the users, because of the nature of drug use, would soon be wanting something stronger and there would be a demand for legalizing other drugs, or "hard" narcotics such as heroin.

Many people feel that marihuana is a special case. They argue that it is not addictive and no more harmful than nicotine or alcohol. Our society once waged a battle against alcohol and is now waging one against cigarette smoking. The present generation "discovered" marihuana and claims it as its own, much in the way that another generation "discovered" bathtub gin; and for much the same reasons. Both are identified with protest against authority. If marihuana is as harmless as some people claim, it will in time go the way of other similar fads and will not lead its young users into the area of serious, addictive drug use. Only time can really determine the outcome. I am concerned not so much about the use of marihuana as about the casual attitude many of us have toward it.

We need a national commission to go into all phases of the use and misuse of drugs. The police and the public need more knowledge of drugs. There is also the problem of synthetics such as LSD which are produced in the lab. No doubt our

194

technology will come up with future drugs that will make LSD seem like nothing. We need more facts in this field. I would not encourage the use of drugs or favor any scheme, at present, which would legalize even the mildest of them.

In today's society is the primary role of the policeman to provide a service?

Most definitely so. The providing of adequate, intelligent, and competent police service is the primary function of the police today. Fortunately we are fast getting away from the idea of the policeman as a person to be dreaded, an individual who goes around meting out punishment.

I think the country realizes this. The main reason this period is called the time of the policeman is because people realize that the police are in a unique position at this point in our history to perform a function that no other group can. It is not a turning away completely from the policeman's traditional role, but certainly makes a strong impulse in a new direction. Because of this new trend society is beginning to look upon the police officer differently and to respect him more than in the past.

There will of course be stumbling blocks. The American people are reluctant to deal with a problem until it becomes a crisis, and as things cool down the pressure for change lowers; yet the crime rate, I fear, will continue to rise. I fear that the death and destruction on the nation's highways will in time become a massacre. The trend toward police unionization also will continue. Ultimately all these problems must be dealt with. If we have a police structure in America built upon competence, professionalism, and scientific analysis we will have the organization that can do the job.

Index

198

200

HERBERT T. JENKINS

Herbert T. Jenkins was born in Lithonia, Georgia. He attended public schools and then went on to Atlanta Law School. Sworn in as a patrolman in October, 1931, a lieutenant in May, 1942, and a captain in February, 1943, he became chief of the Atlanta Police Department in February, 1947. In 1965 he was President of the International Association of Chiefs of Police. In 1967 he was the only police officer appointed by Lyndon B. Johnson to the President's National Advisory Commission on Civil Disorders.